Benvenuto!

Just Enough
ITALIAN

Just Enough
ITALIAN

HOW TO GET BY AND
BE EASILY UNDERSTOOD

McGraw·Hill

New York   Chicago   San Francisco   Lisbon   London   Madrid   Mexico City
Milan   New Delhi   San Juan   Seoul   Singapore   Sydney   Toronto

The **McGraw·Hill** Companies

Library of Congress Cataloging-in-Publication Data

Ellis, D. L.
    Just enough Italian / D. L. Ellis, C. Mariella ; pronunciation by
Dr. J. Baldwin.
        p.   cm.
    Includes index.
    ISBN 0-07-145140-4

    1. Italian language—Conversation and phrase books—English.
I. Mariella, Cinzia. II. Title.

    PC1121.E55 2004
    458.3'421—dc22   2004061087

17 18 19 20 21 22   DOC   20 19 18 17 16

ISBN: 978-0-07-145140-6
MHID: 0-07-145140-4

McGraw-Hill books are available at special quantity discounts
to use as premiums and sales promotions, or for use in corporate
training programs. For more information, please write to the Director
of Special Sales, Professional Publishing, McGraw-Hill, Two Penn
Plaza, New York, NY 10121-2298. Or contact your local bookstore.

This book is printed on acid-free paper.

Contents

Using This Phrase Book

This phrase book is designed to help you get by in Italy—to get what you need or want. It concentrates on the simplest but most effective way that you can express your needs or desires in an unfamiliar language.

The Contents tells you which section of the book to consult for the phrase you need. The Index has a more detailed list of topics that are covered in this book.

When you have found the correct page, you are given either the exact phrase you need or help in making a suitable sentence. You will also be given help in pronunciation. Especially helpful are the sections that provide the likely responses Italian people will give to your questions.

To practice the basic nuts and bolts of the language further, we have included a "Do It Yourself" section at the end of the book.

The sections "Everyday Expressions," "Shop Talk," and "Public Notices" will be particularly useful, and you can expect to refer to them frequently.

Before you leave for Italy, be sure to contact one of the tourist information offices listed below (see page 14).

Italian National Travel Office
50 North Michigan Avenue
Suite 1046
Chicago, IL 60611
(312) 644-0990

Italian National Travel Office
630 Fifth Avenue
New York, NY 10111
(212) 245-4822

Italian National Travel Office
360 Post Street
Suite 801
San Francisco, CA 94108
(415) 392-6206

A Note on Pronunciation

In the typical Italian phrase book, there is a pronunciation key that tries to teach English-speaking tourists how to correctly pronounce Italian. This is based on the belief that in order to be understood, the tourist must pronounce every word almost like a native speaker would.

The authors of this book set out to devise a more workable and more usable pronunciation system. We considered the fact that it is impossible for an average speaker of English, with no training in phonetics or phonetic transcription, to reproduce the sounds of a foreign language perfectly. Further, we believe that you don't have to have perfect pronunciation in order to make yourself understood in a foreign language. After all, native speakers will take into account that you are visitors to their country; they will most likely feel gratified by your efforts to communicate and will go out of their way to try to understand you. We have also found that visitors to a foreign country are not usually concerned with perfect pronunciation—they just want to get their message across, to communicate!

With this in mind, we have devised a pronunciation system of the utmost simplicity. This system does not attempt to give a tedious, problematic representation of Italian sounds; instead, it uses common English sound and letter combinations that are closest to the sounds of Italian. Since Italian (like English) depends on one syllable in a word being stressed, we have put that stressed syllable in italics.

Practice makes perfect, so it is a good idea to repeat aloud to yourself the phrases you think you're going to use, before you actually use them. This will give you greater confidence and will help you to be understood.

You may want to pronounce Italian as well as possible, of course, and the present system is an excellent way to start. Since it uses only the sounds of English, however, you will very soon need to depart from it as you imitate the sounds you hear an Italian produce and begin to relate them to Italian spelling. Fortunately, Italian poses no problems in this regard, as there is an obvious and consistent relationship between pronunciation and spelling.

Divertitevi! Have fun!

Regions and Major Cities of Italy

Everyday Expressions

- See also "Shop Talk," p. 43.

Hello.	**Buon giorno.** boo·*on jor*·no
Good morning.	**Ciao.** (*friends only*) *chah*·oo
Good evening.	**Buona sera.** boo·*o*·nah *seh*·rah
Good night.	**Buona notte.** boo·*o*·nah *not*·teh
Good-bye.	**Arrivederci.** arreeveh·*dair*·chee
See you later.	**A più tardi.** ah pew *tar*·dee
Yes.	**Sì.** see
Please.	**Per favore.** pair fa·*vo*·reh
Yes, please.	**Sì, grazie.** see *graht*·see·eh
Great!	**Magnifico!** man·*yee*·feeco
Thank you.	**Grazie.** *graht*·see·eh
Thank you very much.	**Molte grazie.** *mol*·teh *graht*·see·eh
That's right.	**Esatto.** eh·*zaht*·to
No.	**No.** no
No, thank you.	**No, grazie.** no *graht*·see·eh
I disagree.	**Non sono d'accordo.** non *so*·no dac·*cor*·do
Excuse me.	**Scusi.** *scoo*·zee
Sorry.	**Mi dispiace.** mee deespee·*ah*·cheh
Don't mention it./That's okay.	**Prego.** *preh*·go
That's good./I like it.	**Va bene.** va *ben*·eh

That's no good./I don't like it.	**Non va bene.** non va *ben*·eh
I know.	**Lo so.** lo so
I don't know.	**Non lo so.** non lo so
It doesn't matter.	**Non importa.** non im·*por*·tah
Where is the restroom, please?	**Dov'è il gabinetto, per favore?** do·*veh* il gabee·*net*·to pair fa·*vo*·reh
How much is that?	**Quanto costa?** *quan*·to *cos*·tah
Is the tip included?	**Il servizio è compreso?** il sair·*vit*·see·o eh com·*prai*·zo
Do you speak English?	**Parla inglese?** *par*·lah in·*glai*·zeh
I'm sorry …	**Mi dispiace…** mee deespee·*ah*·cheh
… I don't speak Italian.	**non parlo italiano.** non *par*·lo italee·*ah*·no
… I only speak a little Italian.	**parlo solo un poco italiano.** *par*·lo *so*·lo oon *po*·co italee·*ah*·no
… I don't understand.	**non capisco.** non ca·*pis*·co
Please, can you …	**Per favore, potrebbe…** pair fa·*vo*·reh po·*treb*·beh
… repeat that?	**ripetere?** ri·*peh*·tereh
… speak more slowly?	**parlare più lentamente?** par·*lah*·reh pew lenta·*men*·teh
… write it down?	**scriverlo?** *scree*·verlo
What is this called in Italian?	**Come si dice questo in italiano?** *co*·meh see *dee*·cheh *ques*·to in italee·*ah*·no

Crossing the Border

Essential Information

- Don't waste your time rehearsing what you're going to say to Passport Control officials—chances are, you won't have to say anything at all, especially if you travel by air.

- It is more useful to check that you have the following documents handy for the trip: passport, airline tickets, money, traveler's checks, insurance documents, driver's license, and car registration documents.

- Look for the following signs.

Alt!	Stop!
Controllo Passaporti	Passport Control
Dogana	Customs
Frontiera	Border
Polizia di Frontiera	Border Police

For additional signs and notices, see p. 109.

- You may be asked routine questions by customs officials, such as those below. If you have to provide personal information, see "Meeting People," p. 5. It is important to know how to say "nothing": **Niente** (nee-*en*-teh).

Routine Questions

Passport?	**Passaporto?** passa·*por*·to
Insurance?	**Assicurazione?** assicoorahtsee·*o*·neh
Registration?	**Libretto di circolazione?** li·*bret*·to dee cheercolahtsee·*o*·neh
Ticket, please.	**Biglietto, prego.** bil·*yet*·to *preh*·go
Do you have anything to declare?	**Ha niente da dichiarare?** ah nee·*en*·teh da dikeeah·*rah*·reh
Where are you going?	**Dove va?** *do*·veh va
How long are you staying?	**Per quanto tempo rimane?** pair *quan*·to *tem*·po ree·*mah*·neh
Where are you coming from?	**Da dove viene?** da *do*·veh vee·*ehn*·eh

4 Crossing the Border

You may also be required to fill out forms that ask for the following information.

cognome	last name
nome	first name
data di nascita	date of birth
luogo di nascita	place of birth
indirizzo	address
nazionalità	nationality
professione	profession
numero di passaporto	passport number
rilasciato a	issued at
firma	signature

Meeting People

• See also "Everyday Expressions," p. 1.

Breaking the Ice

Hello./Good morning.
Buon giorno. (Ciao.)
boo·*on* jor·no (*chah*·oo)

How are you?
Come sta? (Come stai?)
co·meh stah (*co*·meh *stah*·ee)

The expressions in parentheses above should only be used with people you know well.

Pleased to meet you.
Piacere.
peeah·*chair*·eh

I am here …
Sono qui…
so·no quee

… on vacation.
in vacanza.
in va·*cahnt*·sah

… on business.
per affari.
pair af·*fah*·ree

Can I offer you …
Posso offrirle…
pos·so of·*freer*·leh

… a drink?
da bere?
da *bair*·eh

… a cigarette?
una sigaretta?
oo·na siga·*ret*·tah

… a cigar?
un sigaro?
oon *see*·garo

How long are you staying?
Quanto tempo rimane?
quan·to *tem*·po ree·*mah*·neh

Names

What's your name?
Come si chiama?
co·meh see kee·*ah*·mah

My name is _____ .
Mi chiamo _____ .
mee kee·*ah*·mo…

Family

Are you married?	**Lei è sposato** (*male*)/ **sposata** (*female*)? lay eh spo·*zah*·to/spo·*zah*·tah
I am …	**Sono…** *so*·no
… married.	**sposato** (*male*)/**sposata** (*female*). spo·*zah*·to/spo·*zah*·tah
… single.	**celibe** (*male*)/**nubile** (*female*). *cheh*·lee·beh/*noo*·bee·leh
This is …	**Le presento…** leh pre·*zen*·to
… my wife.	**mia moglie.** *mee*·ah *mol*·yeh
… my husband.	**mio marito.** *mee*·o ma·*ree*·to
… my son.	**mio figlio.** *mee*·o *feel*·yo
… my daughter.	**mia figlia.** *mee*·ah *feel*·yah
… my (boy)friend.	**il mio ragazzo.** il *mee*·o ra·*gaht*·so
… my (girl)friend.	**la mia ragazza.** la *mee*·ah ra·*gaht*·sah
… my (male) colleague.	**il mio collega.** il *mee*·o col·*leh*·gah
… my (female) colleague.	**la mia collega.** la *mee*·ah col·*leh*·gah
Do you have any children?	**Lei ha figli?** lay ah *feel*·yee
I have …	**Ho…** o
… one daughter.	**una figlia.** *oo*·na *feel*·yah
… one son.	**un figlio.** oon *feel*·yo
… two daughters.	**due figlie.** *doo*·eh *feel*·yeh
… three sons.	**tre figli.** treh *feel*·yee
No, I don't have children.	**No, non ho figli.** no non o *feel*·yee

Where You Live

Are you …	**Lei è…** lay eh
… Italian?	**italiano** (*male*)/**italiana** (*female*)? italee·*ah*·no/italee·*ah*·nah
… Swiss?	**svizzero** (*male*)/**svizzera** (*female*)? *zveet*·sero/*zveet*·serah
I am …	**Sono…** *so*·no
… American.	**americano** (*male*)/ **americana** (*female*). ameri·*cah*·no/ameri·*cah*·nah

For other nationalities, see p. 122.

I live …	**Abito…** *ah*·beeto
… in Chicago.	**a Chicago.** ah shi·*kah*·go
… in the United States.	**negli Stati Uniti.** *nel*·yee *stah*·tee oo·*nee*·tee

For other countries, see p. 121.

… in the north.	**al nord.** al nord
… in the south.	**al sud.** al sood
… in the east.	**all'est.** al·*lest*
… in the west.	**all'ovest.** al·*lo*·vest
… in the center.	**al centro.** al *chen*·tro

For the Businessman and Businesswoman

I'm from _____ (*company name*).	**Sono della _____.** *so*·no *del*·la…
I have an appointment with _____.	**Ho un appuntamento con _____.** o oon appoonta·*men*·to con…
May I speak to _____?	**Potrei parlare con _____?** po·*tray* par·*lah*·reh con…
Here is my card.	**Ecco il mio biglietto da visita.** *ec*·co il *mee*·o bil·*yet*·to da *vee*·zitah

I'm sorry I'm late.

Mi dispiace, sono in ritardo.
mee deespee·*ah*·cheh *so*·no
in ree·*tar*·do

Can I make another
appointment?

**Potrei fissare un altro
appuntamento?**
po·*tray* fis·*sah*·reh oon *al*·tro
appoonta·*men*·to

I'm staying at the (Paris) Hotel.

Sono all'hotel (Parigi).
so·no allo·*tel* (pa·*ree*·jee)

I'm staying on (St. John's)
Street.

Sto in via (San Giovanni).
sto in *vee*·ah (sahn jo·*vahn*·nee)

Asking Directions

Essential Information

- You will find the names of the following places on shops, maps, and public signs and notices.

What to Say

Excuse me, please.	**Scusi, per favore.** scoo·zee pair fa·vo·reh
How do I get …	**Per andare…** pair an·dah·reh
… to Rome?	**a Roma?** ah ro·mah
… to the Via Nomentana?	**in via Nomentana?** in vee·ah nomen·tah·nah
… to the Hotel Torino?	**all'hotel Torino?** allo·tel to·ree·no
… to the airport?	**all'aeroporto?** alla·airo·por·to
… to the beach?	**alla spiaggia?** al·la spee·ahd·jah
… to the bus station?	**alla stazione degli autobus?** al·la stahtsee·o·neh del·yee ah·oo·toboos
… to downtown?	**in centro?** in chen·tro
… to the historic district?	**al centro storico?** al chen·tro sto·rico
… to the market?	**al mercato?** al mair·cah·to
… to the police station?	**alla stazione di polizia?** al·la stahtsee·o·neh dee poleet·see·ah
… to the port?	**al porto?** al por·to
… to the post office?	**all'ufficio postale?** alloof·fee·cho pos·tah·leh
… to the railway station?	**alla stazione ferroviaria?** al·la stahtsee·o·neh ferrovee·ah·reeah
… to the stadium?	**allo stadio?** al·lo stah·deeo

How do I get ...
Per andare...
pair an·*dah*·reh

... to the tourist information office?
all'ufficio del turismo?
alloof·*fee*·cho del too·*rees*·mo

... to the town hall?
al municipio?
al moo·ni·*chee*·peeo

Is there ... nearby?
C'è... qui vicino?
cheh ... quee vee·*chee*·no

... an art gallery ...
una galleria d'arte
oo·na galle·*ree*·ah *dar*·teh

... a baker's ...
un panificio
oon panee·*fee*·cho

... a bakery ...
una pasticceria
oo·na pasteechair·*ee*·ah

... a bank ...
una banca
oo·na *bahn*·cah

... a bar ...
un bar
oon bar

... a botanical garden ...
un giardino botanico
oon jar·*dee*·no bo·*tah*·neeco

... a bus stop ...
una fermata dell'autobus
oo·na fair·*mah*·tah dellah·*oo*·toboos

... a butcher ...
una macelleria
oo·na machelle·*ree*·ah

... a café ...
un bar
oon bar

... a campsite ...
un campeggio
oon cam·*ped*·jo

... a church ...
una chiesa
oo·na kee·*eh*·zah

... a cinema ...
un cinema
oon *chee*·nemah

... a delicatessen ...
una salumeria
oo·na saloome·*ree*·ah

... a dentist's office ...
un dentista
oon den·*tees*·tah

... a department store ...
un grande magazzino
oon *grahn*·deh magad·*zee*·no

... a disco ...
una discoteca
oo·na disco·*teh*·cah

... a doctor's office ...
uno studio medico
oo·no *stoo*·deeo *meh*·deeco

... a drugstore ...
una farmacia
oo·na farma·*chee*·ah

Is there … nearby?	**C'è… qui vicino?** cheh … quee vee·*chee*·no
… a dry cleaner's …	**una lavanderia a secco** *oo*·na lavande·*ree*·ah ah *sec*·co
… an exchange office …	**un ufficio del cambio** oon oof·*fee*·cho del *cahm*·beeo
… a fish market …	**una pescheria** *oo*·na peske·*ree*·ah
… a garage (*for repairs*) …	**un'autorimessa** oonah·ootoree·*mes*·sah
… a gas station …	**un distributore/benzinaio** oon distriboo·*to*·reh/benzee·*nah*·yo
… a hairdresser's …	**un parrucchiere** oon parrookee·*air*·eh
… a hardware store …	**un negozio di ferramenta** oon ne·*got*·seeo dee ferra·*men*·tah
… a Health and Social Security Office …	**una sezione dell'INAM** *oo*·na setsee·*o*·neh del·*lee*·nahm
… a hospital …	**un ospedale** oon ospe·*dah*·leh
… a hotel …	**un albergo** oon al·*bair*·go
… an ice-cream shop …	**una gelateria** *oo*·na jelate·*ree*·ah
… a laundromat …	**una lavanderia** *oo*·na lavande·*ree*·ah
… a mailbox …	**una buca delle lettere** *oo*·na *boo*·cah *del*·leh *let*·tereh
… a museum …	**un museo** oon moo·*zeh*·o
… a newsstand …	**un'edicola** oone·*dee*·colah
… a nightclub …	**un night** oon night
… a parking garage …	**un parcheggio** oon par·*ked*·jo
… a pastry shop …	**una pasticceria** *oo*·na pasteechair·*ee*·ah
… a public garden (park) …	**un giardino pubblico** oon jar·*dee*·no *poob*·blico
… a public restroom …	**un gabinetto pubblico** oon gabi·*net*·to *poob*·blico
… a restaurant …	**un ristorante** oon risto·*rahn*·teh

Is there ... nearby?	**C'è... qui vicino?** cheh ... quee vee·*chee*·no
... a (snack) bar ...	**un bar** oon bar
... a sports field ...	**un campo sportivo** oon *cahm*·po spor·*tee*·vo
... a supermarket ...	**un supermercato** oon soopairmair·*cah*·to
... a swimming pool ...	**una piscina** *oo*·na pi·*shee*·nah
... a taxi stand ...	**una stazione taxi** *oo*·na stahtsee·*o*·neh *tah*·xi
... a telephone ...	**un telefono** oon tel·*eh*·fono
... a theater ...	**un teatro** oon teh·*ah*·tro
... a tobacco shop ...	**un tabaccaio** oon tabac·*cah*·yo
... a travel agency ...	**un'agenzia di viaggi** oonajent·*see*·ah dee vee·*ahd*·jee
... a vegetable store ...	**un verduraio** oon verdoo·*rah*·yo
... a youth hostel ...	**un ostello per la gioventù** oon os·*tel*·lo pair la joven·*too*
... a zoo ...	**uno zoo** *oo*·no *dzo*·o

Directions

- Asking where a place is, or if a place is nearby, is one thing; making sense of the answer is another. Here are some of the most common directions and replies you will receive.

left	**sinistra** si·*nees*·trah
right	**destra** *des*·trah
straight ahead	**sempre diritto** *sem*·preh dee·*reet*·to
there	**là** lah
first left/right	**la prima a sinistra/destra** la *pree*·mah ah si·*nees*·trah/*des*·trah

second left/right	**la seconda a sinistra/destra** la se·*con*·dah ah si·*nees*·trah/*des*·trah
at the crossroad/intersection	**all'incrocio** alleen·*cro*·cho
at the traffic light	**al semaforo** al se·*mah*·foro
at the traffic circle	**alla rotonda** *al*·la ro·*ton*·dah
at the railway crossing	**al passaggio a livello** al pas·*sahd*·jo ah li·*vel*·lo
It's near/far.	**È vicino/lontano.** eh vee·*chee*·no/lon·*tah*·no
one kilometer	**un chilometro** oon kee·*lo*·metro
two kilometers	**due chilometri** *doo*·eh kee·*lo*·metree
Five minutes …	**Cinque minuti…** *chin*·queh mi·*noo*·tee
… on foot.	**a piedi.** ah pee·*eh*·dee
… by car.	**in macchina.** in *mah*·kee·nah
Take …	**Prenda…** *pren*·dah
… the bus.	**l'autobus.** la·*oo*·toboos
… the streetcar.	**il tram.** il trahm
… the subway.	**la metropolitana.** la metropolee·*tah*·nah
… the train.	**il treno.** il *treh*·no

For public transportation, see p. 100.

The Tourist Information Office

Essential Information

- Most towns and many villages in Italy have a tourist office, run by the regional or local tourist boards. Look for the following signs.

  Ufficio Informazioni Turistiche
  Ente Turismo

- You can also get information from the Touring Club and Automobile Club offices, often indicated by the abbreviations **TCI** (Italian Touring Club) and **ACI** (Italian Automobile Club). ACI also offers help with car repairs and accidents.

- These offices provide free information in the form of leaflets, pamphlets, brochures, lists, transportation schedules, and maps. There may be a charge for some of these, but this is not typical.

- For finding a tourist information office, see p. 10.

What to Say

Please, do you have …	**Per favore, avete…** pair fa·*vo*·reh a·*veh*·teh
… a map of the town?	**una pianta della città?** *oo*·na pee·*ahn*·tah *del*·la chit·*tah*
… a list of bus tours?	**un elenco di gite in autobus?** oon e·*len*·co dee *jee*·teh in ah·*oo*·toboos
… a list of campsites?	**un elenco dei campeggi?** oon e·*len*·co day cam·*ped*·jee
… a list of events?	**un elenco di avvenimenti?** oon e·*len*·co dee avveni·*men*·tee
… a list of hotels?	**un elenco degli alberghi?** oon e·*len*·co *del*·yee al·*bair*·ghee
… a list of restaurants?	**un elenco dei ristoranti?** oon e·*len*·co day risto·*rahn*·tee
… a brochure on the town?	**un opuscolo sulla città?** oon o·*poos*·colo *sool*·la chit·*tah*
… a brochure on the region?	**un opuscolo sulla regione?** oon o·*poos*·colo *sool*·la reh·*jo*·neh
… a train schedule?	**un orario ferroviario?** oon o·*rah*·reeo ferrovee·*ah*·reeo
… a bus schedule?	**un orario degli autobus?** oon o·*rah*·reeo *del*·yee ah·*oo*·toboos

In English, please.	**In inglese, per favore.**
	in in·*glai*·zeh pair fa·*vo*·reh
How much do I owe you?	**Quanto Le devo?**
	quan·to leh *deh*·vo
Can you recommend …	**Mi potrebbe raccomandare…**
	mee po·*treb*·beh raccoman·*dah*·reh
… an inexpensive hotel?	**un albergo non caro?**
	oon al·*bair*·go non *cah*·ro
… an inexpensive restaurant?	**un ristorante non caro?**
	oon risto·*rahn*·teh non *cah*·ro
Can you make a reservation for me?	**Potrebbe prenotare per me?**
	po·*treb*·beh preno·*tah*·reh pair meh

Likely Answers

- When the answer is "no," you should be able to tell by the person's facial expression, tone of voice, or gesture, but there are language clues, such as the following.

No.	**No.**
	no
I'm sorry.	**Mi dispiace.**
	mee deespee·*ah*·cheh
I don't have a list of campsites.	**Non ho un elenco dei campeggi.**
	non o oon e·*len*·co day cam·*ped*·jee
I don't have any more left.	**Non ne ho più.**
	non neh o pew
It's free.	**È gratis.**
	eh *grah*·tis

Accommodations

Hotel

Essential Information

- If you want hotel-type accommodations, look for the following signs.

  Hotel
  Albergo
  Motel (*Two major motel chains are run by ACI and AGIP.*)

- Hotels are divided into five classes (from luxury to tourist class), and **pensioni** (boarding houses) into three classes.

- Lists of hotels and **pensioni** can be obtained from local tourist offices or from the Italian National Travel Office (see p. ix).

- Since the price is displayed in the room itself, you can check it as you are looking at the room before agreeing to stay. The displayed price is for the room itself—per night, not per person. Breakfast is extra and therefore optional.

- Service and VAT (value-added tax) are always included in the price of the room, so tipping is optional.

- Other than breakfast, not all hotels provide meals. A **pensione** always provides meals. Breakfast is continental-style: coffee or tea, with rolls and jam.

- Some form of identification, like a passport or driver's license, is requested when registering at a hotel; the ID is normally kept overnight.

- To ask directions to a hotel, see p. 11.

What to Say

I have a reservation.	**Ho una prenotazione.** o *oo*·na prenotahtsee·*o*·neh
Do you have any vacancies, please?	**Avete delle camere libere, per favore?** a·*veh*·teh *del*·leh *cah*·mereh *lee*·bereh pair fa·*vo*·reh
Can I reserve a room?	**Potrei prenotare una camera?** po·*tray* preno·*tah*·reh *oo*·na *cah*·merah

It's for … **È per…**
eh pair

… one person. **una persona.**
oo·na pair·*so*·nah

… two people. **due persone.**
doo·eh pair·*so*·neh

For numbers, see p. 113.

It's for … **È per…**
eh pair

… one night. **una notte.**
oo·na *not*·teh

… two nights. **due notti.**
doo·eh *not*·tee

… one week. **una settimana.**
oo·na setti·*mah*·nah

… two weeks. **due settimane.**
doo·eh setti·*mah*·neh

I would like … **Vorrei…**
vor·*ray*

… a room … **una camera**
oo·na *cah*·merah

… two rooms … **due camere**
doo·eh *cah*·mereh

… with a single bed. **singola** (*one single bed*)/
singole (*two single beds*).
sin·golah/*sin*·goleh

… with two single beds. **a due letti.**
ah *doo*·eh *let*·tee

… with a double bed. **con un letto matrimoniale.**
con oon *let*·to matrimonee·*ah*·leh

… with a rollaway bed. **con una culla.**
con *oo*·na *cool*·lah

… with a bathroom. **con bagno.**
con *bahn*·yo

… with a shower. **con doccia.**
con *do*·chah

… with a balcony. **con terrazzo.**
con ter·*raht*·so

I would like … **Vorrei…**
vor·*ray*

… full board. **pensione completa.**
pensee·*o*·neh com·*pleh*·tah

I would like …	**Vorrei…** vor·*ray*
… half board.	**mezza pensione.** *med*·za pensee·*o*·neh
… bed and breakfast.	**solo colazione.** *so*·lo colahtsee·*o*·neh
Do you serve meals?	**Servite i pasti?** sair·*vee*·teh ee *pahs*·tee
(At) what time is …	**A che ora è…** ah keh *o*·rah eh
… breakfast?	**la colazione?** la colahtsee·*o*·neh
… lunch?	**il pranzo?** il *prahn*·zo
… dinner?	**la cena?** la *cheh*·nah
How much is it?	**Quanto costa?** *quan*·to *cos*·tah
Can I look at the room?	**Potrei vedere la stanza?** po·*tray* ve·*dair*·eh la *stahn*·zah
I would prefer a room …	**Preferirei una stanza…** preferee·*ray* oo·na *stahn*·zah
… in the front/in the back.	**sul davanti/sul retro.** sool da·*vahn*·tee/sool *reh*·tro
I'd like a quiet room.	**Vorrei una camera tranquilla.** vor·*ray* oo·na *cah*·merah tran·*queel*·lah
Okay, I'll take it.	**Va bene, la prendo.** va *ben*·eh la *pren*·do
No, thanks, I won't take it.	**No, grazie, non la prendo.** no *graht*·see·eh non la *pren*·do
The key to number (10), please.	**Per favore, la chiave del numero (dieci).** pair fa·*vo*·reh la kee·*ah*·veh del *noo*·mero (dee·*eh*·chee)
Please, may I have …	**Per favore, potrei avere…** pair fa·*vo*·reh po·*tray* a·*vair*·eh
… an ashtray?	**un portacenere?** oon porta·*cheh*·nereh
… another blanket?	**un'altra coperta?** oon·*al*·tra co·*pair*·tah

Please, may I have …
Per favore, potrei avere…
  pair fa·*vo*·reh po·*tray* a·*vair*·eh

… a coat hanger?
un attaccapanni?
  oon attacca·*pahn*·nee

… a glass?
un bicchiere?
  oon beekee·*air*·eh

… another pillow?
un altro cuscino?
  oon *al*·tro coo·*shee*·no

… some soap?
del sapone?
  del sa·*po*·neh

… a towel?
un asciugamano?
  oon ashooga·*mah*·no

Come in!
Avanti!
  a·*vahn*·tee

One moment, please!
Un momento, per favore!
  oon mo·*men*·to pair fa·*vo*·reh

Please, can you …
Per favore, potrebbe…
  pair fa·*vo*·reh po·*treb*·beh

… do this laundry/do this
  dry cleaning?
**far lavare questo/far lavare questo
  a secco?**
  far la·*vah*·reh *ques*·to/far la·*vah*·reh
  ques·to ah *sec*·co

… call me at (seven)?
chiamarmi alle (sette)?
  keeah·*mar*·mee *al*·leh (*set*·teh)

… help me with my luggage?
aiutarmi con i bagagli?
  ahyoo·*tar*·mee con ee ba·*gal*·yee

… call me a taxi for (nine)?
chiamarmi un taxi per le (nove)?
  keeah·*mar*·mee oon *tah*·xi pair leh
  (*no*·veh)

For telling time, see p. 115.

The bill, please.
Il conto, per favore.
  il *con*·to, pair fa·*vo*·reh

Is the tip included?
Il servizio è compreso?
  il ser·*vit*·seeo eh com·*prai*·zo

I think this is wrong.
Penso che questo sia sbagliato.
  pen·so keh *ques*·to *see*·ah
  sbal·*yah*·to

May I have a receipt?
Potrei avere la ricevuta?
  po·*tray* a·*vair*·eh la riche·*voo*·tah

At Breakfast

Some more …, please.	**Ancora…, per favore.** an·co·rah … pair fa·vo·reh
… coffee …	**del caffè** del caf·feh
… tea …	**del tè** del teh
… bread …	**del pane** del pah·neh
… butter …	**del burro** del boor·ro
… jam …	**della marmellata** del·la marmel·lah·tah
May I have a boiled egg?	**Potrei avere un uovo alla coque?** po·tray a·vair·eh oon wo·vo al·la coc

Likely Reactions

Do you have any identification, please?	**Ha un documento di riconoscimento, per favore?** ah oon docoo·men·to dee riconoshee·men·to pair fa·vo·reh
What's your name?	**Come si chiama?** co·meh see kee·ah·mah
Sorry, we're full.	**Spiacente, siamo al completo.** speeah·chen·teh see·ah·mo al com·pleh·to
We don't have any rooms left.	**Non ci sono più camere.** non chee so·no pew ca·mereh
Do you want to have a look?	**Vuole vederla?** voo·o·leh ve·dair·lah
How many people is it for?	**Per quante persone?** pair quan·teh pair·so·neh
From (ten o'clock) on.	**Dalle (dieci) in poi.** dal·leh (dee·eh·chee) in poy
From (midday) on.	**Da (mezzogiorno) in poi.** da (medzo·jor·no) in poy

For telling time, see p. 115.

It's (40) euros.	**Sono (quaranta) euro.** so·no (quah·rahn·tah) eh·oo·ro

For numbers, see p. 113.

Camping and Youth Hosteling

Essential Information

CAMPING

- Look for the word **Camping** or **Campeggio** or the sign below.

- Be prepared to pay:

  per person
  for the car (if applicable)
  for the tent or the trailer space
  for electricity
  for a hot shower

- You must provide proof of identity, such as your passport.

- You can obtain lists of campsites from local tourist offices (see p. 14) or from the Italian National Travel Office (see p. ix).

- To rent a space in advance (particularly recommended in July and August), write to the Centro Internazionale Prenotazioni Campeggio, Casella Postale 23, 50041 Calenzano, Italia.

- Some campsites offer discounts to campers with the International Camping Carnet (an ID card that provides access to campgrounds controlled by clubs that belong to one of several international travel associations).

- Camping off-site is permitted except in state forests and national parks. It is always best to ask permission from the landowner.

YOUTH HOSTELS

- Look for the words **Ostello per la Gioventù** or the sign at right.

- You will be asked for your Youth Hostels Association (YHA) card and your passport upon arrival.

- You will have to rent sheets on arrival.

- Food and cooking facilities vary from hostel to hostel, and you may have to help with domestic chores.

- In peak season it is advisable to book beds in advance; your stay will be limited to a maximum of three consecutive nights per hostel.

- Apply to the Italian Tourist Board (E.N.I.T.) or to the local tourist office in Italy (see p. 14) for lists of youth hostels and details of regulations for hostelers.

- For buying or replacing camping equipment, see p. 41.

What to Say

I have a reservation.	**Ho una prenotazione.** o *oo*·na prenotahtsee·*o*·neh
Do you have any vacancies?	**Avete dei posti liberi?** a·*veh*·teh day *pos*·tee *lee*·beree
It's for …	**È per…** eh pair
… one adult/one person …	**un adulto/una persona** oon a·*dool*·to/*oo*·na pair·*so*·nah
… two adults/two people …	**due adulti/due persone** *doo*·eh a·*dool*·tee/*doo*·eh pair·*so*·neh
… and one child.	**e un bambino.** eh oon bam·*bee*·no
… and two children.	**e due bambini.** eh *doo*·eh bam·*bee*·nee
It's for …	**È per…** eh pair
… one night.	**una notte.** *oo*·na *not*·teh

Do you have …	**Avete…**
	a·*veh*·teh
… a shop?	**un negozio?**
	oon ne·*got*·seeo
… a swimming pool?	**una piscina?**
	oo·na pi·*shee*·nah

For food shopping, see p. 47.

For eating and drinking out, see p. 66.

Where are …	**Dove sono…**
	do·veh *so*·no
… the toilets?	**i gabinetti?**
	ee gabi·*net*·tee
… the showers?	**le docce?**
	leh *do*·cheh
… the trash cans?	**le pattumiere?**
	leh pattoomee·*air*·eh
(At) what time must one …	**A che ora si deve…**
	ah keh *o*·rah see *deh*·veh
… go to bed?	**andare a dormire?**
	an·*dah*·reh ah dor·*mee*·reh
… get up?	**alzare?**
	alt·*sah*·reh
Please, do you have …	**Per favore, avete…**
	pair fa·*vo*·reh a·*veh*·teh
… a bottle opener?	**un apribottiglie?**
	oon apreebot·*teel*·yeh
… a broom?	**una scopa?**
	oo·na *sco*·pah
… a can opener?	**un apriscatole?**
	oon aprees·*cah*·toleh
… any dish detergent?	**del sapone per lavare i piatti?**
	del sa·*po*·neh pair la·*vah*·reh
	ee pee·*aht*·tee
… a towel?	**uno straccio per asciugare?**
	oo·no *strah*·cho pair ashoo·*gah*·reh
… a fork?	**una forchetta?**
	oo·na for·*ket*·tah
… a frying pan?	**una padella per friggere?**
	oo·na pa·*del*·lah pair *freed*·jereh
… an iron?	**un ferro da stiro?**
	oon *fer*·ro da *stee*·ro

Please, do you have …	**Per favore, avete…** pair fa·*vo*·reh a·*veh*·teh
… a knife?	**un coltello?** oon col·*tel*·lo
… a plate?	**un piatto?** oon pee·*aht*·to
… a refrigerator?	**un frigorifero?** oon frigo·*ree*·fero
… a saucepan?	**una pentola?** *oo*·na *pen*·tolah
… any soap powder?	**della polvere per lavare?** *del*·la *pol*·vereh pair la·*vah*·reh
… a teaspoon?	**un cucchiaino?** oon cookeeah·*ee*·no
The bill, please.	**Il conto, per favore.** il *con*·to, pair fa·*vo*·reh

Problems

The faucet …	**Il rubinetto…** il roobi·*net*·to
The light …	**La luce…** la *loo*·cheh
The razor outlet …	**La spina per il rasoio…** la *spee*·nah pair il ra·*zoy*·o
The shower …	**La doccia…** la *do*·chah
The toilet …	**Il gabinetto…** il gabi·*net*·to
… is not working.	**non funziona.** non foontsee·*o*·nah
My camping gas has run out.	**La bombola del gas è finita.** la *bom*·bolah del gahz eh fee·*nee*·tah

Likely Reactions

Do you have any identification?	**Ha un documento di riconoscimento?** ah oon docoo·*men*·to dee riconoshee·*men*·to
Your membership card, please.	**La sua tessera, per favore.** la *soo*·ah *tes*·serah pair fa·*vo*·reh
What's your name?	**Come si chiama?** *co*·meh see kee·*ah*·mah

Sorry, we're full.	**Spiacente, siamo al completo.** speeah·*chen*·teh see·*ah*·mo al com·*pleh*·to
How many people is it for?	**Per quante persone?** pair *quan*·teh pair·*so*·neh
How many nights is it for?	**Per quante notti?** pair *quan*·teh *not*·tee
It's (eight) euros …	**Sono (otto) euro…** *so*·no (*ot*·to) eh·oo·ro
… per day/per night.	**al giorno/per notte.** al *jor*·no/pair *not*·teh

For numbers, see p. 113.

Rented Lodging

Essential Information

- If you are looking for lodging to rent, look for the following words in advertising and on signs.

Da affittare/Affittasi	For rent
Appartamento/Alloggio	Apartment
Villa	Villa
Villetta/Villino	Cottage
Chalet	Chalet

- For arranging details of your rental, see "Hotel," p. 16.

- If you rent on the spot, you need to know the following words.

deposit	**il deposito** il deh·*po*·zeeto
key	**la chiave** la kee·*ah*·veh

- Having arranged your accommodation and arrived with the key, check the basic amenities that you take for granted at home.

- *Electricity:* Voltage? You may need an adapter for razors and small appliances brought from home.

  Learn how to turn the lights on and off.

- *Gas:* Municipal (natural) gas or bottled gas? Butane gas must be kept indoors, and propane gas must be kept outdoors.

- *Stove:* Don't be surprised to find the grill inside the oven (or no grill at all); a lid covering the burners that lifts up to form a backsplash; or a mixture of two gas burners and two electric burners.
- *Toilet:* Sewer drainage or septic tank? Don't flush disposable diapers or similar materials down the toilet if you have a septic tank.
- *Water:* Locate the shut-off valve. Check the faucets and plugs—they may not operate the way you are used to.
- *Windows:* Learn how to open and close windows and shutters.
- *Insects:* Is an insecticide spray provided? If not, buy one.
- *Equipment:* See p. 41 for buying or replacing equipment.
- You will probably deal with a real estate agent, but find out whom to contact in an emergency; it may be a neighbor who is renting the lodging to you.

What to Say

My name is _____ .	**Mi chiamo _____.** mee kee·*ah*·mo…
I'm staying at _____ .	**Sono al _____.** *so*·no al…
They have cut off …	**Hanno interrotto…** *ahn*·no inter·*rot*·to
… the electricity.	**l'elettricità.** lelettreechee·*tah*
… the gas.	**il gas.** il gahz
… the water.	**l'acqua.** *lah*·quah
Is there … in the area?	**C'è… nella zona?** cheh … *nel*·la *dzo*·nah?
… an electrician …	**un elettricista** oon elettree·*chis*·tah
… a gas repairman …	**un addetto al gas** oon ad·*det*·to al gahz
… a plumber …	**un idraulico** oon ee·drah·*oo*·lico
Where is …	**Dov'è…** do·*veh*
… the furnace?	**la caldaia?** la cal·*dah*·yah

Where is …
Dov'è…
do·*veh*

… the fuse box?
la scatola dei fusibili?
la *scah*·tolah day foo·*zee*·bilee

… the water heater?
lo scaldaacqua?
lo *scahl*·dah *ah*·quah

… the water shut-off valve?
il rubinetto principale?
il roobi·*net*·to princhee·*pah*·leh

Is there …
C'è…
cheh

… municipal gas?
il gas di città?
il gahz dee chit·*tah*

… bottled gas?
gas in bombola?
gahz in *bom*·bolah

… a septic tank?
una fossa settica?
oo·na *fos*·sah *set*·teecah

… central heating?
il riscaldamento centrale?
il riscalda·*men*·to chen·*trah*·leh

The burner …
Il fornello…
il for·*nel*·lo

The hair dryer …
L'asciugacapelli…
lashoogaca·*pel*·lee

The heating system …
Il riscaldamento…
il riscalda·*men*·to

The iron …
Il ferro da stiro…
il *fer*·ro da *stee*·ro

The pilot light …
La fiammella spia…
la feeah·*mel*·lah *spee*·ah

The refrigerator …
Il frigorifero…
il frigo·*ree*·fero

The telephone …
Il telefono…
il te·*le*·fono

The toilet …
Il gabinetto…
il gabi·*net*·to

The washing machine …
La lavatrice…
la lava·*tree*·cheh

The water heater …
Lo scaldaacqua…/Il boiler…
lo *scahl*·dah *ah*·quah/il *boy*·ler

… is not working.
non funziona.
non foontsee·*o*·nah

Where can I get …
Dove posso trovare…
do·veh *pos*·so tro·*vah*·reh

… an adapter for this?
una spina per questo?
oo·na *spee*·nah pair *ques*·to

Where can I get …	**Dove posso trovare…** *do*·veh *pos*·so tro·*vah*·reh
… a fuse?	**un fusibile?** oon foo·*zee*·bileh
… a light bulb?	**una lampadina?** *oo*·na lampa·*dee*·nah
… insecticide spray?	**una bombola insetticida?** *oo*·na *bom*·bolah insetti·*chee*·dah
… a tank of butane gas?	**una bombola di gas butano?** *oo*·na *bom*·bolah dee gahz boo·*tah*·no
… a tank of propane gas?	**una bombola di gas propano?** *oo*·na *bom*·bolah dee gahz pro·*pah*·no
The drain …	**Lo scarico…** lo *scah*·rico
The sink …	**Il lavandino…** il lavan·*dee*·no
The toilet …	**Il gabinetto…** il gabi·*net*·to
… is stopped up.	**è otturato.** eh ottoo·*rah*·to
The gas is leaking.	**Il gas perde.** il gahz *pair*·deh
Can you repair it right away?	**Può ripararlo subito?** poo·*o* ripa·*rar*·lo *soo*·beeto
When can you repair it?	**Quando potrà ripararlo?** *quan*·do po·*trah* ripa·*rar*·lo
How much do I owe you?	**Quanto Le devo?** *quan*·to leh *de*·vo
When is the garbage collected?	**Quando raccolgono i rifiuti?** *quan*·do rac·*col*·gono ee ree·*few*·tee

Likely Reactions

What's your name?	**Come si chiama?** *co*·meh see kee·*ah*·mah
What's your address?	**Il suo indirizzo?** il *soo*·o indee·*rit*·so
There is a shop …	**C'è un negozio…** cheh oon ne·*got*·seeo
… in town.	**in città.** in chit·*tah*
… in the village.	**in paese.** in pah·*eh*·zeh

I can't come …	**Non posso venire…** non *pos*·so ve·*nee*·reh
… today.	**oggi.** *od*·jee
… this week.	**questa settimana.** *ques*·tah setti·*mah*·nah
… until Monday.	**fino a lunedì.** *fee*·no ah loone·*dee*
I can come …	**Posso venire…** *pos*·so ve·*nee*·reh
… on Tuesday.	**martedì.** marte·*dee*
… whenever you want.	**quando vuole.** *quan*·do voo·o·leh
Every day.	**Ogni giorno.** *on*·yee *jor*·no
Every other day.	**Un giorno sì e uno no.** oon *jor*·no see eh *oo*·no no
On Wednesday.	**Tutti i mercoledì.** *toot*·tee ee maircole·*dee*

For days of the week, see p. 117.

General Shopping

The Drugstore

Essential Information

- Look for the word **Farmacia** or the sign at right.
- Prescription medicines are available only at a drugstore.
- Some nonprescription drugs can be bought at a supermarket or department store.
- Try the drugstore before going to the doctor; pharmacists are usually qualified to treat minor health problems.

- Drugstores take turns staying open all night and on Sundays. A notice on the door titled **Farmacie di turno** or **Servizio notturno** gives the hours of operation.
- Some toiletries can also be bought at a **profumeria**, but they will be more expensive there.
- For finding a drugstore, see p. 10.

What to Say

I would like …	**Vorrei…**
	vor·*ray*
… some Alka-Seltzer.	**dell'Alka-Seltzer.**
	del·*lal*·ka *selt*·ser
… some antiseptic.	**dell'antisettico.**
	del·lanti·*set*·tico
… some aspirin.	**dell'aspirina.**
	del·laspi·*ree*·nah
… some bandages.	**delle bende.**
	del·leh *ben*·deh
… some Band-Aids.	**del cerotto.**
	del che·*rot*·to
… some cotton balls.	**del cotone.**
	del co·*to*·neh
… some eyedrops.	**del collirio.**
	del col·*leer*·yo

I would like …	**Vorrei…** vor·*ray*
… some foot powder.	**del talco per piedi.** del *tahl*·co pair pee·*eh*·dee
… some gauze.	**della garza.** *del*·la *gard*·zah
… some inhalant.	**dell'inalante.** dellina·*lahn*·teh
… some insect repellent.	**della crema anti-insetti.** *del*·la *creh*·mah antee·in·*set*·tee
… some lip balm.	**della crema per le labbra.** *del*·la *creh*·mah pair leh *lahb*·brah
… some nose drops.	**delle gocce per il naso.** *del*·leh *go*·cheh pair il *nah*·zo
… some throat lozenges.	**delle pastiglie per la gola.** *del*·leh pas·*teel*·yeh pair la *go*·lah
… some Vaseline.	**della vaselina.** *del*·la vaze·*lee*·nah
I would like something for …	**Vorrei qualcosa per…** vor·*ray* qual·*co*·zah pair
… bites.	**morsicature.** morseeca·*too*·reh
… burns.	**bruciature/scottature.** broocha·*too*·reh/scotta·*too*·reh
… a cold.	**il raffreddore.** il raffred·*do*·reh
… constipation.	**stitichezza.** stiti·*ket*·sah
… a cough.	**la tosse.** la *tos*·seh
… cracked skin.	**screpolature.** screpola·*too*·reh
… diarrhea.	**diarrea.** deeah·*reh*·ah
… an earache.	**mal d'orecchie.** mal dorre·*kee*·eh
… flu.	**influenza.** infloo·*ent*·sah
… car/sea/air sickness.	**mal d'auto/di mare/d'aereo.** mal dah·*oo*·to/dee *mah*·reh/ da·*air*·eh·o
… sore gums.	**mal di gengive.** mal dee jen·*jee*·veh

I would like something for …	**Vorrei qualcosa per…**
	vor·*ray* qual·*co*·zah pair
… sprains.	**distorsioni.**
	distorsee·*o*·nee
… stings.	**punture.**
	poon·*too*·reh
… sunburn.	**scottature da sole.**
	scotta·*too*·reh da *so*·leh
I need …	**Avrei bisogno di…**
	av·*ray* bee·*zon*·yo dee
… some baby food.	**cibi per bambini.**
	chee·bee pair bam·*bee*·nee
… some contraceptives.	**contraccettivi.**
	contrachet·*tee*·vee
… some deodorant.	**deodorante.**
	deh·odo·*rahn*·teh
… some disposable diapers.	**pannolini per bambini.**
	panno·*lee*·nee pair bam·*bee*·nee
… some hand cream.	**crema per le mani.**
	creh·mah pair leh *mah*·nee
… some Kleenex.	**fazzoletti di carta.**
	fahtso·*let*·tee dee *car*·tah
… some lipstick.	**un rossetto.**
	oon ros·*set*·to
… some make-up remover.	**latte detergente.**
	lah·teh deter·*jen*·teh
… some razor blades.	**lamette per rasoio.**
	la·*met*·teh pair ra·*zoy*·o
… some safety pins.	**spille di sicurezza.**
	speel·leh dee seecoo·*ret*·sah
… some sanitary napkins.	**assorbenti igienici.**
	assor·*ben*·tee ee·*jen*·eechee
… some shaving cream.	**crema da barba.**
	creh·mah da *bar*·bah
… some soap.	**sapone.**
	sa·*po*·neh
… some suntan lotion/oil.	**crema/olio solare.**
	creh·mah/*ol*·yo so·*lah*·reh
… some talcum powder.	**borotalco.**
	boro·*tahl*·co
… some tampons.	**tampax.**
	tam·pax
… some toilet paper.	**carta igienica.**
	car·tah ee·*jen*·eecah

I need …	**Avrei bisogno di…**
	av·*ray* bee·*zon*·yo dee
… some toothpaste.	**dentifricio.**
	dentee·*free*·cho

For other essential expressions, see "Shop Talk," p. 43.

Vacation Items

Essential Information

- Here are other places to shop at and signs to look for.

Libreria-cartoleria	Stationery store
Tabaccheria	Tobacco shop
Articoli da regalo	Presents
Foto-ottico	Photography items

- The main department stores in Italy are the following.

Coin
Rinascente
Upim

What to Say

Where can I buy …?	**Dove posso comprare…?**
	do·veh *pos*·so com·*prah*·reh
I would like …	**Vorrei…**
	vor·*ray*
… a beach ball.	**un pallone da spiaggia.**
	oon pal·*lo*·neh da spee·*ahd*·jah
… a bucket.	**un secchiello.**
	oon sehkee·*el*·lo
… an English newspaper.	**un giornale inglese.**
	oon jor·*nah*·leh in·*glai*·zeh
… some envelopes.	**delle buste.**
	del·leh *boos*·teh
… a guidebook.	**una guida.**
	oo·na *guee*·dah
… a handbag/purse.	**una borsa.**
	oo·na *bor*·sah
… a map (of the area).	**una pianta (della zona).**
	oo·na pee·*ahn*·tah (*del*·la *dzo*·nah)
… a parasol.	**un parasole.**
	oon para·*so*·leh

I would like …	**Vorrei…** vor·*ray*
… some postcards.	**delle cartoline.** *del*·leh carto·*lee*·neh
… a shovel.	**una paletta.** *oo*·na pa·*let*·tah
… a straw hat.	**un cappello di paglia.** oon cap·*pel*·lo dee *pahl*·yah
… a suitcase.	**una valigia.** *oo*·na va·*lee*·jah
… some sunglasses.	**degli occhiali da sole.** *del*·yee okee·*ah*·lee da *so*·leh
… an umbrella.	**un ombrello.** oon om·*brel*·lo
… some writing paper.	**della carta da lettere.** *del*·la *car*·tah da *let*·tereh
I would like … [*show the camera*]	**Vorrei…** vor·*ray*
… a roll of color film …	**una pellicola a colori** *oo*·na pel·*lee*·colah ah co·*lo*·ree
… for prints.	**per fotografie.** pair fotograh·*fee*·eh
… with 12/24/36 exposures.	**da dodici/ventiquattro/trentasei pose.** da *do*·deechee/ventee·*quaht*·tro/ trenta·*say* po·zeh
… some batteries.	**delle batterie.** *del*·leh batte·*ree*·yeh
This camera is broken.	**Questa macchina fotografica è rotta.** *ques*·ta *mah*·kee·nah foto·*grah*·feecah eh *rot*·tah
The film is stuck.	**Il film è bloccato.** il feelm eh bloc·*cah*·to
Please, can you …	**Per favore, potrebbe…** pair fa·*vo*·reh po·*treb*·beh
… develop/print this?	**sviluppare/stampare questo?** zveeloop·*pah*·reh/stam·*pah*·reh *ques*·to
… load the camera?	**caricare la macchina fotografica?** caree·*cah*·reh la *mah*·kee·nah foto·*grah*·feeca

For other essential expressions, see "Shop Talk," p. 43.

The Tobacco Shop

Essential Information

- Tobacco is sold where you see the sign at right.
- For asking if there is a tobacco shop nearby, see p. 12.
- All tobacco shops sell postage stamps and salt.
- A tobacco shop is sometimes part of a café/bar, a stationery store (**cartoleria**), or a newsstand.

What to Say

A pack of cigarettes …	**Un pacchetto di sigarette…** oon pah·*ket*·to dee siga·*ret*·teh
… with filters.	**con filtro.** con *feel*·tro
… without filters.	**senza filtro.** *sent*·sah *feel*·tro
… king size.	**formato lungo.** for·*mah*·to *loon*·go
… menthol.	**al mentolo.** al men·*to*·lo
Those up there …	**Quelle là sopra…** *quel*·leh la *so*·prah
… on the right.	**a destra.** ah *des*·trah
… on the left.	**a sinistra.** ah si·*nees*·trah
These. [*point*]	**Queste.** *ques*·teh

Cigarettes, please.	**Sigarette, per favore.**
	siga·*ret*·teh pair fa·*vo*·reh
100/200/300 / two packs.	**Cento/duecento/**
	trecento / due pacchetti.
	chen·to/doo·eh·*chen*·to/
	treh·*chen*·to / *doo*·eh pah·*ket*·tee
Do you have ...	**Avete...**
	a·*veh*·teh
... English cigarettes?	**sigarette inglesi?**
	siga·*ret*·teh in·*glai*·zee
... American cigarettes?	**sigarette americane?**
	siga·*ret*·teh ameri·*cah*·neh
... English pipe tobacco?	**tabacco inglese da pipa?**
	ta·*bahc*·co in·*glai*·zeh da *pee*·pah
... American pipe tobacco?	**tabacco americano da pipa?**
	ta·*bahc*·co ameri·*cah*·no da *pee*·pah
... rolling tobacco?	**tabacco sciolto?**
	ta·*bahc*·co *shol*·to
... a package of pipe tobacco?	**un pacchetto di tabacco da pipa?**
	oon pah·*ket*·to dee ta·*bahc*·co
	da *pee*·pah
That one up there ...	**Quello là sopra...**
	quel·lo la *so*·prah
... on the right.	**a destra.**
	ah *des*·trah
... on the left.	**a sinistra.**
	ah si·*nees*·trah
This one. [*point*]	**Questo.**
	ques·to
Those.	**Quelli.**
	quel·lee
A cigar, please.	**Un sigaro, per favore.**
	oon *see*·garo pair fa·*vo*·reh
Some cigars.	**Dei sigari.**
	day *see*·garee
A box of matches.	**Una scatola di cerini.**
	oo·na *scah*·tolah dee che·*ree*·nee
A package of pipe cleaners.	**Un pacchetto di filtri per pipa.**
	oon pah·*ket*·to dee *feel*·tree pair
	pee·pah
A package of flints.	**Un pacchetto di pietrine.**
	oon pah·*ket*·to dee pee·eh·*tree*·neh

Lighter fluid, please.

Della benzina per accendino, per favore.
del·la ben·*zee*·nah pair atchen·*dee*·no pair fa·*vo*·reh

For other essential expressions, see "Shop Talk," p. 43.

Buying Clothes

Essential Information

· Look for the following signs.

Abbigliamento per signora   Women's clothes
Abbigliamento da uomo   Men's clothes
Calzature   Shoes

· Don't buy clothing without being measured first or trying the item on.

· Don't rely solely on conversion charts of clothing sizes (see p. 127).

· If you are buying clothing for someone else, take his or her measurements with you.

· The department stores **Coin**, **Rinascente**, and **Upim** all sell clothes and shoes.

What to Say

I would like ...

Vorrei...
vor·*ray*

... a belt.

una cintura.
oo·na chin·*too*·rah

... a bikini.

un due pezzi.
oon doo·eh *pet*·see

... a bra.

un reggiseno.
oon redjee·*seh*·no

... a swimming cap.

una cuffia (da bagno).
oo·na *coof*·feeah (da *bahn*·yo)

... a ski cap.

un berretto (da sci).
oon ber·*ret*·to (da shee)

... a cardigan.

un golf.
oon golf

... a coat.

un cappotto.
oon cap·*pot*·to

... a dress.

un vestito.
oon ves·*tee*·to

I would like …	**Vorrei…** vor·*ray*
… a hat.	**un cappello.** oon cap·*pel*·lo
… a jacket.	**una giacca.** *oo*·na *jahc*·cah
… a jumper.	**una maglia.** *oo*·na *mahl*·yah
… a nightgown.	**una camicia da notte.** *oo*·na ca·*mee*·chah da *not*·teh
… a pair of pajamas.	**un pigiama.** oon pid·*jah*·mah
… a V-neck pullover.	**un pullover.** oon pool·*lo*·ver
… a raincoat.	**un impermeabile.** oon imperme·*ah*·bileh
… a shirt.	**una camicia.** *oo*·na ca·*mee*·chah
… a skirt.	**una gonna.** *oo*·na *gon*·nah
… a suit.	**un completo.** oon com·*pleh*·to
… a swimsuit.	**un costume da bagno.** oon cos·*too*·meh da *bahn*·yo
… a T-shirt.	**una maglietta di cotone.** *oo*·na mal·*yet*·tah dee co·*to*·neh
… a windbreaker.	**una giacca a vento.** *oo*·na *jahc*·cah ah *ven*·to
I would like a pair of …	**Vorrei un paio di…** vor·*ray* oon *pah*·yo dee
… briefs. [*women*]	**mutandine.** mootan·*dee*·neh
… gloves.	**guanti.** *guan*·tee
… jeans.	**jeans.** jeenz
… shorts.	**pantaloni corti.** panta·*lo*·nee *cor*·tee
… socks (short/long).	**calze (corte/lunghe).** *calt*·seh (*cor*·teh/*loon*·geh)
… stockings.	**calze di nylon.** *calt*·seh dee *nah*·ee·lon
… tights.	**collant.** col·*lahn*

I would like a pair of …	**Vorrei un paio di…**
	vor·*ray* oon *pah*·yo dee
… trousers.	**pantaloni.**
	panta·*lo*·nee
… underwear. [*men*]	**slip da uomo.**
	slip da *wo*·mo
… shoes.	**scarpe.**
	scar·peh
… canvas shoes.	**scarpe di tela.**
	scar·peh dee *teh*·lah
… sandals.	**sandali.**
	sahn·dalee
… beach sandals.	**sandali da spiaggia.**
	sahn·dalee da spee·*ahd*·jah
… dress shoes.	**scarpe eleganti.**
	scar·peh ele·*gahn*·tee
… boots.	**stivali.**
	stee·*vah*·lee
… loafers.	**mocassini.**
	mocas·*see*·nee
My size is _____.	**Porto il numero _____.**
	por·to il *noo*·mero…

For numbers, see p. 113.

For clothing sizes, see p. 127.

Can you measure me, please?	**Può prendermi la misura,**
	per favore?
	poo·*o pren*·der·mee la mee·*zoo*·rah
	pair fa·*vo*·reh
Can I try it on?	**Posso provare?**
	pos·so pro·*vah*·reh
It's for a present.	**È per un regalo.**
	eh pair oon re·*gah*·lo
These are the measurements …	**Queste sono le misure…**
[*show written measurements*]	*ques*·teh *so*·no leh mee·*zoo*·reh
collar	**colletto**
	col·*let*·to
bust	**petto**
	pet·to
chest	**torace**
	to·*rah*·cheh
waist	**vita**
	vee·tah

hip	**fianchi** fee·*ahn*·kee
leg	**gamba** *gahm*·bah
Do you have something …	**Avete qualcosa…** a·*veh*·teh qual·*co*·zah
… in black?	**in nero?** in *neh*·ro
… in blue?	**in blu?** in bloo
… in brown?	**in marrone?** in mar·*ro*·neh
… in gray?	**in grigio?** in *greed*·jo
… in green?	**in verde?** in *vair*·deh
… in pink?	**in rosa?** in *ro*·zah
… in red?	**in rosso?** in *ros*·so
… in white?	**in bianco?** in bee·*ahn*·co
… in yellow?	**in giallo?** in *jahl*·lo
… in this color? [*point*]	**in questo colore?** in *ques*·to co·*lo*·reh
… in cotton?	**in cotone?** in co·*to*·neh
… in denim?	**in jeans?** in jeenz
… in leather?	**in pelle?** in *pel*·leh
… in nylon?	**in nylon?** in *nah*·ee·lon
… in suede?	**in pelle scamosciata?** in *pel*·leh scamo·*shah*·tah
… in wool?	**in lana?** in *lah*·nah
… in this material? [*point*]	**in questo tessuto?** in *ques*·to tes·*soo*·to

For other essential expressions, see "Shop Talk," p. 43.

Replacing Equipment

Essential Information

- Look for the following shops and signs.

Elettricista	Electrical items
Ferramenta	Hardware
Elettrodomestici	Household appliances
Articoli per la casa	Household goods
Drogheria	Grocery (household cleaning items)

- In the supermarket, look for the following sign.

Articoli casalinghi	Household goods

- For asking directions to a shop, see p. 9.
- At a campsite, try its shop first.

What to Say

Do you have …	**Avete…**
	a·*veh*·teh
… an adapter? [*show appliance*]	**una spina a riduzione?**
	oo·na *spee*·nah ah ridootsee·*o*·neh
… a tank of butane gas?	**una bombola di gas butano?**
	oo·na *bom*·bolah dee gahz boo·*tah*·no
… a tank of propane gas?	**una bombola di gas propano?**
	oo·na *bom*·bolah dee gahz pro·*pah*·no
… a bottle opener?	**un apribottiglie?**
	oon apreebot·*teel*·yeh
… a can opener?	**un apriscatole?**
	oon aprees·*cah*·toleh
… a clothesline?	**una corda per stendere?**
	oo·na *cor*·dah pair *sten*·dereh
… a corkscrew?	**un cavatappi?**
	oon cavat·*tahp*·pee
… a brush for dishes?	**uno spazzolino per piatti?**
	oo·no spatso·*lee*·no pair pee·*ah*·tee
… any dishwashing detergent?	**del sapone liquido per piatti?**
	del sa·*po*·neh *lee*·quido pair pee·*ah*·tee
… any disinfectant?	**del disinfettante?**
	del disinfet·*tahn*·teh

Do you have …	**Avete…** a·*veh*·teh
… any disposable cups?	**dei bicchieri da buttare?** day beekee·*air*·ee da boot·*tah*·reh
… any disposable plates?	**dei piatti da buttare?** day pee·*aht*·tee da boot·*tah*·reh
… a flashlight?	**una torcia elettrica?** *oo*·na *tor*·chah eh·*let*·treecah
… any forks?	**delle forchette?** *del*·leh for·*ket*·teh
… a fuse? [*show the one* *to be replaced*]	**un fusibile?** oon foo·*zee*·bileh
… insecticide spray?	**uno spray insetticida?** *oo*·no spray insettee·*chee*·dah
… any knives?	**dei coltelli?** day col·*tel*·lee
… a light bulb? [*show the one* *to be replaced*]	**una lampadina?** *oo*·na lampa·*dee*·nah
… a roll of paper towels?	**un rotolo di carta da cucina?** oon *ro*·tolo dee *car*·tah da coo·*chee*·nah
… a plastic bucket?	**un secchio in plastica?** oon *seh*·keeoh in *plahs*·teecah
… a plastic pan?	**un recipiente di plastica?** oon recheepee·*en*·teh dee *plahs*·teecah
… a scouring pad?	**una paglietta abrasiva?** *oo*·na pal·*yet*·tah abra·*see*·vah
… any soap powder?	**della polvere da lavare?** *del*·la *pol*·vereh da la·*vah*·reh
… a sponge?	**una spugna?** *oo*·na *spoon*·yah
… any string?	**dello spago?** *del*·lo *spah*·go
… any tent pegs?	**dei picchetti da tenda?** day pi·*ket*·tee da *ten*·dah
… a towel?	**uno straccio per asciugare?** *oo*·no *strah*·cho pair ashoo·*gah*·reh
… a universal plug (for a sink)?	**un tappo (per lavandino)?** oon *tahp*·po (pair lavan·*dee*·no)
… a wrench?	**una chiave inglese?** *oo*·na kee·*ah*·veh in·*glai*·zeh

For other essential expressions, see "Shop Talk," p. 43.

Shop Talk

Essential Information

- Italy no longer uses the *lira*; it uses euro currency instead.
- Euro coins are in the following denominations: 1, 2, 5, 10, 20, and 50 cents; 1 and 2 euros.
- Euro bills are in the following denominations: €5, €10, €20, €50, €100, and €500.
- Important weights and measures follow.

50 grams	**cinquanta grammi**
	chin·*quan*·tah *grahm*·mee
100 grams	**cento grammi**
	chen·to *grahm*·mee
½ kilo	**mezzo chilo**
	med·zo *kee*·lo
1 kilo	**un chilo**
	oon *kee*·lo
2 kilos	**due chili**
	doo·eh *kee*·lee
½ liter	**mezzo litro**
	med·zo *lee*·tro
1 liter	**un litro**
	oon *lee*·tro
2 liters	**due litri**
	doo·eh *lee*·tree

For numbers, see p. 113.

- You may see the colloquial expressions **etto** (100 grams) or **all'etto** (per 100 grams) on price tags.
- In small shops, don't be surprised if customers, as well as shop assistants, say "hello" and "good-bye" to you.

Customer

Hello./Good morning.	**Buon giorno.**
	boo·*on jor*·no
Good afternoon. [*after 3 P.M.*]	**Buona sera.**
	boo·*o*·na *seh*·rah
Good-bye.	**Arrivederla.**
	arreeve·*dair*·lah

I am just looking.	**Guardo soltanto.** *guar·*do sol·*tahn·*to
Excuse me.	**Mi scusi.** mee *scoo·*zee
How much is this/that?	**Quanto costa questo/quello?** *quan·*to *cos·*tah *ques·*to/*quel·*lo
What is that?	**Che cos'è quello?** keh co·*zeh* quel·lo
What are those?	**Che cosa sono quelli?** keh *co·*zah *so·*no *quel·*lee
Is there a discount?	**C'è uno sconto?** cheh *oo·*no *scon·*to
I'd like that, please.	**Vorrei quello, per favore.** vor·*ray* quel·lo pair fa·*vo·*reh
Not that.	**Non quello.** non *quel·*lo
Like that.	**Come quello.** *co·*meh *quel·*lo
That's enough, thank you.	**Basta così, grazie.** *bahs·*tah co·*zee graht·*see·eh
More, please.	**Ancora, per favore.** an·*co·*rah pair fa·*vo·*reh
Less than that.	**Meno di così.** *meh·*no dee co·*zee*
That's fine./Okay.	**Va bene.** va *ben·*eh
I won't take it, thank you.	**Non lo prendo, grazie.** non lo *pren·*do graht·see·eh
It's not right.	**Non va bene.** non va *ben·*eh
Thank you very much.	**Molte grazie.** *mol·*teh graht·see·eh
Do you have something …	**Avete qualcosa…** a·*veh·*teh qual·*co·*zah
… better?	**di meglio?** dee *mel·*yo
… cheaper?	**di meno caro?** dee *meh·*no *cah·*ro
… different?	**di diverso?** dee dee·*vair·*so
… larger?	**di più grande?** dee pew *grahn·*deh
… smaller?	**di più piccolo?** dee pew *pic·*colo

(At) what time do you …   **A che ora…**
    ah keh *o*·rah

… open?   **aprite?**
    a·*pree*·teh

… close?   **chiudete?**
    kee·oo·*deh*·teh

Can I have a bag, please?   **Posso avere una borsa, per favore?**
    pos·so a·*vair*·eh *oo*·na *bor*·sah
    pair fa·*vo*·reh

Can I have a receipt?   **Posso avere la ricevuta?**
    pos·so a·*vair*·eh la riche·*voo*·tah

Do you take …   **Accettate…**
    achet·*taht*·teh

… American money?   **soldi americani?**
    sol·dee ameri·*cah*·nee

… traveler's checks?   **traveler's checks?**
    tra·velairz checks

… credit cards?   **carte di credito?**
    car·teh dee *creh*·deeto

I would like …   **Vorrei…**
    vor·*ray*

… one like that.   **uno di quelli.**
    oo·no dee *quel*·lee

… two like that.   **due di quelli.**
    doo·eh dee *quel*·lee

Shop Assistant

Can I help you?   **È da servire?**
    eh da ser·*veer*·eh?

What would you like?   **Che cosa desidera?**
    keh *co*·zah deh·*zee*·derah

Will that be all?   **È tutto?**
    eh *toot*·to

Is that all?   **Basta così?**
    bahs·tah co·*zee*

Anything else?   **Nient'altro?**
    nee·en·*tahl*·tro

Would you like it wrapped?   **Glielo incarto?**
    l·yee·*el*·o in·*car*·to

Sorry, I have no more.   **Mi dispiace non ne ho più.**
    mee deespee·*ah*·cheh non neh
    o pew

I haven't got any (more).   **Non ne abbiamo (più).**
    non neh ahbee·*ah*·mo (pew)

How many do you want?

Quanti ne desidera?
  quan·tee neh deh·*zee*·derah

How much do you want?

Quanto ne vuole?
  quan·to neh voo·*o*·leh

Is that enough?

È abbastanza?
  eh ahbah·*stahnt*·sah

Shopping for Food

Bread

Essential Information

- For finding a bakery, see p. 10.
- Here are key words to look for.

Panetteria	Bakery
Panificio	Bread (*usually baked and sold on the premises*)
Panettiere	Baker
Pane	Bread

- Nearly all supermarkets sell bread.
- Opening times vary slightly from shop to shop but are generally 9 A.M.–1 P.M. AND 3:30 P.M.–7:30 P.M. Most bakers open earlier than other shops and are closed one day a week; the day varies from town to town.
- Although large and small loaves of bread are available, rolls are very popular. It is important to note that bread is usually bought by *weight*, not size.
- Bakeries often stock other groceries, particularly milk. There is no milk delivery service in Italy, and the dairy (**latteria**) is fast disappearing.

What to Say

Some bread, please.	**Del pane, per favore.**
	del *pah*·neh pair fa·*vo*·reh
A loaf (like that).	**Una pagnotta (così).**
	oo·na pan·*yot*·tah (co·*zee*)
A large one.	**Una grande.**
	oo·na *grahn*·deh
A small one.	**Una piccola.**
	oo·na *pic*·colah
A bread roll.	**Un panino.**
	oon pah·*nee*·no

250 grams of …	**Duecentocinquanta grammi di…**
	dooeh·chento·chin·*quan*·tah
	grahm·mee dee
½ kilo of …	**Mezzo chilo di…**
	med·zo *kee*·lo dee
1 kilo of …	**Un chilo di…**
	oon *kee*·lo dee
… bread.	**pane.**
	pah·neh
… white bread.	**pane bianco.**
	pah·neh bee·*ahn*·co
… whole wheat bread.	**pane integrale.**
	pah·neh inte·*grah*·leh
… bread rolls.	**panini.**
	pah·*nee*·nee
… crispy bread sticks.	**grissini.**
	gris·*see*·nee
Two loaves.	**Due pagnotte.**
	doo·eh pan·*yot*·teh
Four bread rolls.	**Quattro panini.**
	quaht·tro pah·*nee*·nee

For other essential expressions, see "Shop Talk," p. 43.

Cakes

Essential Information

- Here are key words to look for.

Pasticceria	Cake shop
Pasticciere	Pastry maker
Paste/Dolci	Cakes, pastries, sweets

- For finding a pastry shop, see p. 11.

- A **bar-pasticceria** is a place to buy cakes and have a drink.

- Since Italians eat very little for breakfast, they often go to a bar for a mid-morning snack.

- Most bars have only a few tables and charge more for waiter service. See "Ordering a Drink," p. 66.

What to Say

- Types of cakes vary from region to region, but there is typically a variety of cookies and small cream-filled pastries called **paste fresche**. These are bought by weight, and it is best to point to the selection you prefer.

100 grams of …	**Cento grammi di…** *chen*·to *grahm*·mee dee
200 grams of …	**Duecento grammi di…** dooeh·*chen*·to *grahm*·mee dee
½ kilo of …	**Mezzo chilo di…** *med*·zo *kee*·lo dee
… cream-filled pastries.	**paste fresche.** *pahs*·teh *fres*·keh
… cookies.	**biscotti.** bis·*cot*·tee
A variety, please.	**Misto, per favore.** *mees*·to pair fa·*vo*·reh

Larger pastries and cakes may be bought individually.

A cake (like that), please.	**Una torta (così), per favore.** *oo*·na *tor*·tah (co·*zee*) pair fa·*vo*·reh
An (apple) tart.	**Una crostata (di mele).** *oo*·na cro·*stah*·tah (dee *meh*·leh)
A doughnut.	**Un bombolone.** oon bombo·*lo*·neh
A brioche.	**Una brioche.** *oo*·na bree·*osh*

For other essential expressions, see "Shop Talk," p. 43.

Ice Cream and Sweets

Essential Information

- Here are key words to look for.

Gelati	Ice cream
Gelateria/Cremeria	Ice-cream parlor
Pasticceria	Pastry shop

- The sign **Gelati-produzione propria** means that the ice cream is made daily on the premises and is particularly good.

- The best-known ice-cream brands are the following.

Alemagna	**Chiavacci**
Algida	**Motta**
Besana	**Sammontana**

- Every **gelateria** and **cremeria** has its own specialties, which are either described on menus or displayed on posters.
- Specialties vary from region to region.
- Pre-packaged sweets are also available in supermarkets, bars, and bakeries.

What to Say

A … ice cream, please.	**Per favore, un gelato…** pair fa·*vo*·reh oon je·*lah*·to
… chocolate …	**al cioccolato.** al chocco·*lah*·to
… lemon …	**al limone.** al lee·*mo*·neh
… nougat …	**al torroncino.** al torron·*chee*·no
… peach …	**alla pesca.** *al*·la *pes*·cah
… pistachio …	**al pistacchio.** al pis·*tah*·keeo
… strawberry …	**alla fragola.** *al*·la *frah*·golah
… vanilla …	**alla crema.** *al*·la *creh*·mah
One euro's worth.	**Da un euro.** da oon *eh*·oo·ro
A single cone. [*specify flavor as above*]	**Un cono.** oon *co*·no
Two single cones.	**Due coni.** *doo*·eh *co*·nee
A double-dip cone.	**Un cono a due gusti.** oon *co*·no ah *doo*·eh *goos*·tee
Two double-dip cones.	**Due coni a due gusti.** *doo*·eh *co*·nee ah *doo*·eh *goos*·tee
A mixed cone.	**Un cono misto.** oon *co*·no *mees*·to

A cup.	**Una coppa.**
	oo·na *cop*·pah
A popsicle.	**Un ghiacciolo.**
	oon gheeah·*cho*·lo
A package of …	**Un pacchetto di…**
	oon pah·*ket*·to dee
100 grams of …	**Cento grammi di…**
	chen·to *grahm*·mee dee
200 grams of …	**Duecento grammi di…**
	dooeh·*chen*·to *grahm*·mee dee
… chewing gum.	**cicles.**
	cheec·lehz
… chocolates.	**cioccolatini.**
	choccola·*tee*·nee
… mints.	**caramelle alla menta.**
	cara·*mel*·le *al*·la *men*·tah
… sweets.	**caramelle.**
	cara·*mel*·leh
… toffees.	**caramelle mou.**
	cara·*mel*·leh moo

For other essential expressions, see "Shop Talk," p. 43.

In the Supermarket

Essential Information

- Here are key words to look for.

  | **Supermercato** | Supermarket |
  | **Supermercato-alimentari** | Food supermarket |

- Here are the supermarket chains found in most parts of Italy.

Coop	**Standa**
Garosci	**Upim**
Pam	

- Here are common signs at supermarkets.

Entrata	Entrance
Uscita	Exit
Vietato l'ingresso	No entrance
Cassa	Cash register (checkout)
Offerta speciale	Special offer
Carrelli	Carts

- Supermarket hours vary but are generally 9 A.M.–12:30 P.M. and 3:30 P.M.–7:30 P.M.

- For nonfood items, see "Replacing Equipment," p. 41.

- It is usually not necessary to say anything in a supermarket, but you should ask if you don't see what you want.

What to Say

Excuse me, please.	**Mi scusi, per favore.** mee *scoo*·zee pair fa·*vo*·reh
Where is …	**Dov'è…** do·*veh*
… the bread?	**il pane?** il *pah*·neh
… the butter?	**il burro?** il *boor*·ro
… the cheese?	**il formaggio?** il for·*mahd*·jo
… the chocolate?	**il cioccolato?** il chocco·*lah*·to
… the coffee?	**il caffè?** il caf·*feh*
… the cooking oil?	**l'olio per friggere?** *lol*·yo pair *freed*·jereh
… the canned fish?	**il pesce in scatola?** il *peh*·sheh in *scah*·tolah
… the fresh fish?	**il pesce fresco?** il *peh*·sheh *fres*·co
… the canned fruit?	**la frutta sciroppata?** la *froot*·tah sheerop·*pah*·tah
… the fruit?	**la frutta?** la *froot*·tah
… the jam?	**la marmellata?** la marmel·*lah*·tah
… the meat?	**la carne?** la *car*·neh
… the milk?	**il latte?** il *laht*·teh
… the mineral water?	**l'acqua minerale?** *lah*·quah mine·*rah*·leh
… the pasta?	**la pasta?** la *pahs*·tah

Where is …	**Dov'è…**
	do·*veh*
… the produce section?	**il reparto verdure?**
	il re·*par*·to ver·*doo*·reh
… the salt?	**il sale?**
	il *sah*·leh
… the sugar?	**lo zucchero?**
	lo *dzoo*·kero
… the tea?	**il tè?**
	il teh
… the vinegar?	**l'aceto?**
	la·*cheh*·to
… the wine?	**il vino?**
	il *vee*·no
… the yogurt?	**lo yogurt?**
	lo *yo*·gurt
Where are …	**Dove sono…**
	do·veh *so*·no
… the cookies?	**i biscotti?**
	ee bee·*scot*·tee
… the eggs?	**le uova?**
	leh *wo*·vah
… the canned foods?	**i cibi in scatola?**
	ee *chee*·bee in *scah*·tolah
… the frozen foods?	**i surgelati?**
	ee soorje·*lah*·tee
… the fruit juices?	**i succhi di frutta?**
	ee *soo*·kee dee *froot*·tah
… the potato chips?	**le patatine?**
	leh pata·*tee*·neh
… the seafood?	**i frutti di mare?**
	ee *froot*·tee dee *mah*·reh
… the soft drinks?	**le analcoliche?**
	leh anal·*co*·leekeh
… the sweets?	**i dolci?**
	ee *dol*·chee

For other essential expressions, see "Shop Talk," p. 43.

Picnic Food

Essential Information

· Here are key words to look for.

    Salumeria/Salumi/Gastronomia   Delicatessen

· In these shops, you can buy a wide variety of food, such as ham, salami, cheese, olives, appetizers, sausages, and freshly made carry-out dishes. Specialties vary from region to region.

· Here's a guide to the amount of prepared salad to buy.

    2–3 ounces/70 grams per person, if eaten as an appetizer to a substantial meal
    3–4 ounces/100 grams per person, if eaten as the main course of a picnic-style meal

What to Say

One slice of …	**Una fetta di…** *oo*·na *fet*·tah dee
Two slices of …	**Due fette di…** *doo*·eh *fet*·teh dee
… bacon.	**pancetta.** pan·*chet*·tah
… ham (raw/cooked).	**prosciutto (crudo/cotto).** pro·*shoot*·to (*croo*·do/*cot*·to)
… meat loaf.	**polpettone arrosto.** polpet·*to*·neh ar·*ros*·to
… pork roast.	**arrosto di maiale.** ar·*ros*·to dee mah·*yah*·leh
… roast beef.	**arrosto.** ar·*ros*·to
… salami (raw/cooked).	**salame (crudo/cotto).** sa·*lah*·meh (*croo*·do/*cot*·to)
… tongue.	**lingua.** *lin*·guah
… veal with mayonnaise.	**vitello tonnato.** vee·*tel*·lo ton·*nah*·to

100 grams of …	**Cento grammi di…**
	*chen·*to *grahm·*mee dee
150 grams of …	**Centocinquanta grammi di…**
	chento·chin·*quan·*tah *grahm·*mee dee
200 grams of …	**Duecento grammi di…**
	dooeh·*chen·*to *grahm·*mee dee
300 grams of …	**Trecento grammi di…**
	treh·*chen·*to *grahm·*mee dee
… frankfurter salad.	**insalata di würsteln.**
	insa·*lah·*tah dee *woor·*steln
… prawn salad.	**insalata di gamberetti.**
	insa·*lah·*tah dee gam·be·*ret·*tee
… rice salad.	**insalata di riso.**
	insa·*lah·*tah dee *ree·*zo
… Russian salad.	**insalata russa.**
	insa·*lah·*tah *roos·*sah
… seafood salad.	**insalata di mare.**
	insa·*lah·*tah dee *mah·*reh
… tuna and olive salad.	**insalata di tonno e olive.**
	insa·*lah·*tah dee *ton·*no eh o·*lee·*veh

You might also like to try some of the following foods.

green olives	**olive verdi**
	o·*lee·*veh *vair·*dee
stuffed green olives	**olive verdi ripiene**
	o·*lee·*veh *vair·*dee rip·*yeh·*neh
black olives	**olive nere**
	o·*lee·*veh *nair·*eh
baked black olives	**olive nere al forno**
	o·*lee·*veh *nair·*eh al *for·*no
mushrooms preserved in oil	**funghetti sott'olio**
	foon·*ghet·*tee sot·*tol·*yo
peppers preserved in oil	**peperoni sott'olio**
	pepe·*ro·*nee sot·*tol·*yo
roasted peppers	**peperoni arrosto**
	pepe·*ro·*nee ar·*ros·*to
stuffed peppers	**peperoni ripieni**
	pepe·*ro·*nee rip·*yeh·*nee
stuffed tomatoes	**pomodori ripieni**
	pomo·*do·*ree rip·*yeh·*nee
stuffed onions	**cipolle ripiene**
	chi·*pol·*leh rip·*yeh·*neh

eggplant cooked in tomato sauce and parmesan cheese
melanzane in parmigiana
  melan·*zah*·neh in parmi·*jah*·nah

zucchini cooked in oil and vinegar, sage, and garlic
zucchini in carpione
  dzoo·*kee*·nee in carpee·*o*·neh

stuffed zucchini
zucchini ripieni
  dzoo·*kee*·nee rip·*yeh*·nee

fried potatoes
patatine fritte
  pata·*tee*·neh *freet*·teh

meat lasagna
lasagne al forno
  la·*zahn*·yeh al *for*·no

small, flat semolina "dumplings" with butter and parmesan cheese
gnocchi alla romana
  n·*yo*·kee *al*·la ro·*mah*·nah

potato "dumplings" with melted fontina cheese
gnocchi alla fontina
  n·*yo*·kee *al*·la fon·*tee*·nah

large tubular pasta stuffed with meat or with spinach and cheese
cannelloni ripieni
  cannel·*lo*·nee rip·*yeh*·nee

vegetable pie
torta di verdura
  tor·ta dee ver·*doo*·rah

a puff pastry pie with spinach, eggs, and herbs
torta pasqualina
  tor·ta pasquah·*lee*·nah

parmesan (a hard, sharp cheese used in cooking)
parmigiano
  parmi·*jah*·no

a mild, fresh white cheese made from goat's milk
robiola
  robee·*o*·lah

a hard, sharp cheese, eaten fresh or grated when mature
pecorino
  peco·*ree*·no

a very bland, soft white curd cheese made from ewe's milk
ricotta
  ri·*cot*·tah

a rich Alpine cheese, usually melted and used in cooking
fontina
  fon·*tee*·nah

a hard, yellow cow's-milk cheese, displayed hanging up
provolone
  provo·*lo*·neh

a blue-veined cheese with a rich, soft texture
gorgonzola
  gor·gont·*so*·lah

a white, flavorless curd cheese, to be eaten very fresh
mozzarella
  mot·sah·*rel*·lah

For other essential expressions, see "Shop Talk," p. 43.

Fruits and Vegetables

Essential Information

- Here are key words to look for.

Frutta	Fruit
Verdura	Vegetables
Primizie	"Early" (fresh) produce
Alimentari	Grocery
Mercato	Market

- If possible, buy fruit and vegetables at a market, where they are cheaper and fresher than in stores and shops. Open-air markets are held once or twice a week in most areas (sometimes daily in large towns), usually in the mornings.

- It is customary for you to choose your own fruit and vegetables at the market (and in some shops) and for the attendant to weigh and price them. You must take your own shopping bag; paper and plastic bags are not typically provided.

- Weight guide: One kilo of potatoes serves six people.

What to Say

250 grams of …	**Duecentocinquanta grammi di…** dooeh·chento·chin·*quan*·tah *grahm*·mee dee
½ kilo (about 1 pound) of …	**Mezzo chilo di…** *med*·zo *kee*·lo dee
1 kilo of …	**Un chilo di…** oon *kee*·lo dee
2 kilos of …	**Due chili di…** *doo*·eh *kee*·lee dee
… apples.	**mele.** *meh*·leh
… bananas.	**banane.** ba·*nah*·neh
… cherries.	**ciliegie.** chil·*yeh*·jeh
… grapes (white/black).	**uva (bianca/nera).** *oo*·vah (bee·*ahn*·cah/*nair*·ah)
… oranges.	**arance.** a·*rahn*·cheh

250 grams of ...	**Duecentocinquanta grammi di...** dooeh·chento·chin·*quan*·tah *grahm*·mee dee
½ kilo (about 1 pound) of ...	**Mezzo chilo di...** *med*·zo *kee*·lo dee
1 kilo of ...	**Un chilo di...** oon *kee*·lo dee
2 kilos of ...	**Due chili di...** *doo*·eh *kee*·lee dee
... peaches.	**pesche.** *pes*·keh
... pears.	**pere.** *pair*·eh
... plums.	**prugne.** *proon*·yeh
... strawberries.	**fragole.** *frah*·goleh
... artichokes.	**carciofi.** car·*cho*·fee
... carrots.	**carote.** ca·*ro*·teh
... eggplant.	**melanzane.** melan·*zah*·neh
... green beans.	**fagiolini.** fadjo·*lee*·nee
... leeks.	**porri.** *por*·ree
... mushrooms.	**funghi.** *foon*·ghee
... onions.	**cipolle.** chi·*pol*·leh
... peas.	**piselli.** pee·*zel*·lee
... peppers (green/red).	**peperoni (verdi/rossi).** pepe·*ro*·nee (*vair*·dee/*ros*·see)
... potatoes.	**patate.** pah·*tah*·teh
... spinach.	**spinaci.** spee·*nah*·chee
... tomatoes.	**pomodori.** pomo·*do*·ree
... zucchini.	**zucchini.** dzoo·*kee*·nee

A pineapple, please.	**Un ananas, per favore.** oon *ah*·nanas pair fa·*vo*·reh
A grapefruit.	**Un pompelmo.** oon pom·*pel*·mo
A melon.	**Un melone.** oon me·*lo*·neh
A watermelon.	**Un'anguria.** oonan·*goor*·eeah
A bunch of …	**Un mazzetto di…** oon mat·*set*·to dee
… parsley.	**prezzemolo.** pret·*seh*·molo
… radishes.	**ravanelli.** ravah·*nel*·lee
A head of garlic.	**Una testa d'aglio.** *oo*·na *tes*·tah *dal*·yo
Some lettuce.	**Dell'insalata.** dellinsa·*lah*·tah
A (head of) cauliflower.	**Un cavolfiore.** oon cavolfee·*o*·reh
A (head of) cabbage.	**Un cavolo.** oon *cah*·volo
A stick of celery.	**Un sedano.** oon se·*dah*·no
A cucumber.	**Un cetriolo.** oon chetree·*o*·lo
Like that, please.	**Come quello, per favore.** *co*·meh *quel*·lo pair fa·*vo*·reh

The following fruits and vegetables may not be familiar to you.

soft, sweet winter fruit, like a large tomato	**cachi** *kah*·kee
medlars (small, slightly sour fruit, orange in color and juicy)	**nespole** *nes*·poleh
cardoons (the top stalks of the thistle artichoke)	**cardi** *car*·dee
fennel (crunchy vegetable with aniseed flavor)	**finocchi** fee·*no*·kee
small-leafed red salad with a slightly bitter flavor	**radicchio rosso** ra·*dee*·keeo *ros*·so

For other essential expressions, see "Shop Talk," p. 43.

Meat

Essential Information

- Here are key words to look for.

Macellaio	Butcher
Macelleria	Butcher's shop

- Butchers, especially in small towns and villages, often display a white sheet outside their shops for identification.

- Weight guide: 4–6 ounces/110–170 grams of meat serves one person.

- The accompanying figures can help you make sense of labels on counters and supermarket displays. Translations are often unhelpful, and you won't need to say the Italian word.

- Mutton and lamb are sold and eaten only around Easter.

What to Say

To buy a roast, first indicate the type of meat, then say how many people it is for.

Some beef, please.	**Del manzo, per favore.** del *mahn*·zo pair fa·*vo*·reh
Some lamb.	**Dell'agnello.** del·lan·*yel*·lo
Some pork.	**Del maiale.** del mah·*yah*·leh
Some veal.	**Del vitello.** del vee·*tel*·lo
A roast …	**Un arrosto…** oon ar·*ros*·to
… for two people.	**per due persone.** pair *doo*·eh pair·*so*·neh
… for four people.	**per quattro persone.** pair *quaht*·tro pair·*so*·neh
… for six people.	**per sei persone.** pair say pair·*so*·neh

For steak, liver, and heart, the same method of ordering applies.

Some steak, please.	**Della bistecca, per favore.** *del*·la bee·*stec*·cah pair fa·*vo*·reh
Some liver.	**Del fegato.** del *feh*·gato

Beef **Manzo**

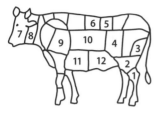

1 Stinco
2 Muscolo
3 Girello
4 Coscia, noce, rosa
5 Lombo, filetto
6 Costata
7 Guancia, testa
8 Collo
9 Polpa di spalla
10 Costata
11 Punta di petto
12 Pancia

Veal **Vitello**

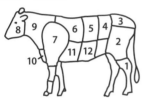

1 Ossobuco
2 Cosciotto, magatello, noce
3 Codino
4 Lombata, nodini, costolette scamone
5 Filetto
6 Copertina di spalla
7 Spalla, capello del prete, fusello
8 Testina
9 Collo
10 Fiocco di petto
11 Punta di petto
12 Pancetta

Pork **Maiale**

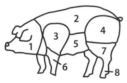

1 Testina
2 Coste, lombata, lonza, filetto
3 Spalla, prosciutto di spalla
4 Coscia, prosciutto di mezzo
5 Petto, pancetta
6 Cosciotto
7 Coscia, zampone
8 Piedino

Lamb, kid **Agnello, capretto**

1 Testina, collo
2 Sella, costolette
3 Cosciotto
4 Spalla
5 Petto

Some kidneys.	**Dei rognoni.** day ron·*yo*·nee
Some heart.	**Del cuore.** del *kwo*·reh
Some sausages.	**Delle salsicce.** *del*·leh sal·*see*·cheh
Some ground meat …	**Della carne tritata…** *del*·la *car*·neh tree·*tah*·tah
… for three people.	**per tre persone.** pair treh pair·*so*·neh
… for five people.	**per cinque persone.** pair *chin*·queh pair·*so*·neh

For chops, order in the following way.

Two veal chops.	**Due fettine di vitello.** *doo*·eh fet·*tee*·neh dee vee·*tel*·lo
Three pork chops.	**Tre braciole di maiale.** treh brah·*cho*·leh dee mah·*yah*·leh
Four lamb chops.	**Quattro costolette d'agnello.** *quaht*·tro costo·*let*·teh dahn·*yel*·lo
Five beef chops.	**Cinque fettine di manzo.** *chin*·queh fet·*tee*·neh dee *mahn*·zo

You may also want the following.

A chicken.	**Un pollo.** oon *pol*·lo
A rabbit.	**Un coniglio.** oon co·*neel*·yo
A tongue.	**Una lingua.** *oo*·na *lin*·guah

For other essential expressions, see "Shop Talk," p. 43.

Please, can you …	**Per favore, potrebbe…** pair fa·*vo*·reh po·*treb*·beh
… clean it?	**pulirlo?** poo·*leer*·lo
… grind it?	**tritarlo?** tree·*tar*·lo
… dice it?	**tagliarlo a pezzetti?** tal·*yar*·lo ah pet·*set*·tee
… trim the fat?	**togliere il grasso?** tol·*yeh*·reh il *grahs*·so

Fish

Essential Information

- Look for the following signs.

  Pescheria   Fish shop
  Mercato del pesce   Fish market

- Another sign to look for is **Frutti di mare** (shellfish).

- Large supermarkets usually have a fresh fish department.

- Weight guide: A minimum of 9 ounces/250 grams of fish on the bone
  serves one person. Use the following table as a guide.

1/2 kilo/500 grams	for 2 people
1 kilo	for 4 people
1 1/2 kilos	for 6 people

What to Say

Purchase large fish and small shellfish by weight.

1/2 kilo of …	**Mezzo chilo di…** *med·*zo *kee·*lo dee
1 kilo of …	**Un chilo di…** oon *kee·*lo dee
1 1/2 kilos of …	**Un chilo e mezzo di…** oon *kee·*lo eh *med·*zo dee
… anchovies.	**acciughe.** ah·*choo·*geh
… cod.	**merluzzo.** mer·*loot·*so
… eel.	**anguilla.** an·*gueel·*lah
… mussels.	**muscoli/cozze.** *moos·*colee/*cot·*seh
… octopus.	**polpo/polipo.** *pol·*po/*po·*lee·po
… oysters.	**ostriche.** *os·*treekeh
… prawns.	**gamberi.** *gahm·*beree
… red mullet.	**triglie.** *treel·*yeh
… sardines.	**sardine.** sar·*dee·*neh

½ kilo of …	**Mezzo chilo di…**
	med·zo kee·lo dee
1 kilo of …	**Un chilo di…**
	oon *kee·lo dee*
1½ kilos of …	**Un chilo e mezzo di…**
	oon *kee·lo* eh *med·zo* dee
… scampi.	**scampi.**
	scahm·pee
… shrimp.	**gamberetti.**
	gambe·*ret·tee*
… small squid.	**calamaretti.**
	calama·*ret·tee*
… squid.	**calamari.**
	cala·*mah·ree*

Some large fish can be purchased by the slice.

One slice of …	**Una fetta di…**
	*oo·*na *fet·*tah dee
Two slices of …	**Due fette di…**
	*doo·*eh *fet·*teh dee
Six slices of …	**Sei fette di…**
	say *fet·*teh dee
… cod.	**merluzzo.**
	mer·*loot·*so
… dogfish.	**palombo.**
	pa·*lom·*bo
… swordfish.	**pescespada.**
	pesheh·*spah·*dah
… fresh tuna.	**tonno fresco.**
	*ton·*no *fres·*co

For some shellfish and "frying pan" fish, specify the number you want.

One bass, please.	**Un branzino, per favore.**
	oon brahn·*zee·*no pair fa·*vo·*reh
One cod.	**Un merluzzo.**
	oon mer·*loot·*so
One crab.	**Un granchio.**
	oon *grahn·*keeo
One gilthead.	**Un'orata.**
	oono·*rah·*tah
One lobster.	**Un'aragosta.**
	oonara·*gos·*tah
One mullet.	**Un cefalo.**
	oon *cheh·*falo

One red mullet.	**Una triglia.** *oo*·na *treel*·yah
One sole.	**Una sogliola.** *oo*·na *sol*·yolah
One trout.	**Una trota.** *oo*·na *tro*·tah

For other essential expressions, see "Shop Talk," p. 43.

Please, can you …	**Per favore, potrebbe…** pair fa·*vo*·reh po·*treb*·beh
… remove the heads?	**tagliare le teste?** tal·*yah*·reh leh *tes*·teh
… clean them?	**pulirli?** poo·*leer*·lee
… fillet them?	**tagliarli in filetti?** tal·*yar*·lee in fee·*let*·tee

Eating and Drinking Out

Ordering a Drink

Essential Information

- Here are the places to ask for (see p. 10).

Bar/Bar-pasticceria	Drinks and cakes
Caffè/Birreria	Beer and snacks

- By law, the price list of drinks (**Listino prezzi**) must be displayed somewhere in the bar.

- There is waiter service in some cafés, but you can drink at the bar or counter, which is cheaper. In the latter case, you first pay at the cash register (**cassa**), then take the receipt (**scontrino**) to the bar and give your order.

- Service is normally included in the bill (**servizio compreso**); if not, you should tip 10% to 15% of the bill.

- Bars and cafés serve both alcoholic and nonalcoholic drinks.

- There are no licensing hours, and children are allowed in.

- Italians drink a range of aperitifs (**aperitivi**) and digestives (**digestivi**). Their names vary from region to region. Most of the aperitifs are types of vermouth—red or white, sweet or dry—made by companies such as Campari, Punt e Mes, and Martini. The digestives may be made from almonds, fruit, or herbs and are often thick and syrupy.

What to Say

I'll have …, please.	**Prendo, per favore,…**
	pren·do pair fa·vo·reh
… black coffee (small and strong) …	**un caffè.**
	oon caf·feh
… black coffee (less strong) …	**un caffè lungo.**
	oon caf·feh loon·go
… coffee with a splash of cream …	**un caffè macchiato.**
	oon caf·feh mahkee·ah·to
… milky coffee (*usually for breakfast*) …	**un caffellatte.**
	oon caffeh·laht·teh
… a cappuccino …	**un cappuccino.**
	oon cappoo·chee·no

I'll have …, please.	**Prendo, per favore,…** *pren*·do pair fa·*vo*·reh
… tea …	**un tè** oon teh
… with milk …	**al latte.** al *laht*·teh
… with lemon …	**al limone.** al lee·*mo*·neh
… a glass of milk …	**un bicchiere di latte.** oon beekee·*air*·eh dee *laht*·teh
… hot chocolate …	**una cioccolata calda.** *oo*·na chocco·*lah*·tah *cahl*·dah
… mineral water …	**una minerale.** *oo*·na mine·*rah*·leh
… iced coffee …	**una granita di caffè.** *oo*·na grah·*nee*·tah dee caf·*feh*
… a Coca-Cola …	**una Coca cola.** *oo*·na *co*·ca *co*·la
… an orange soda …	**un'aranciata.** oonaran·*chah*·tah
… lemonade …	**una limonata.** *oo*·na leemo·*nah*·tah
… fresh lemon juice …	**una spremuta di limone.** *oo*·na spre·*moo*·tah dee lee·*mo*·neh
… fresh orange juice …	**una spremuta d'arancia.** *oo*·na spre·*moo*·tah da·*rahn*·chah
… fresh grapefruit juice …	**una spremuta di pompelmo.** *oo*·na spre·*moo*·tah dee pom·*pel*·mo
… pineapple juice …	**un succo di frutta all'ananas.** oon *sooc*·co dee *froot*·tah al·*ah*·nanas
… peach juice …	**un succo di frutta alla pesca.** oon *sooc*·co dee *froot*·tah *al*·la *pes*·cah
… a beer …	**una birra.** *oo*·na *beer*·rah
… a dark beer …	**una birra scura.** *oo*·na *beer*·rah *scoo*·rah

A glass of …	**Un bicchiere di…** oon beekee-*air*-eh dee
Two glasses of …	**Due bicchieri di…** *doo*-eh beekee-*air*-ee dee
… red wine.	**vino rosso.** *vee*-no *ros*-so
… white vine.	**vino bianco.** *vee*-no bee-*ahn*-co
… rosé …	**rosé** ro-*zeh*
… dry.	**secco.** *sec*-co
… sweet.	**dolce.** *dol*-cheh
A bottle of …	**Una bottiglia di…** *oo*-na bot-*teel*-yah dee
… sparkling wine.	**spumante.** spoo-*mahn*-teh
… champagne.	**champagne.** sham-*pahn*-yeh
A whisky …	**Un whisky…** oon *wis*-kee
… with ice.	**con ghiaccio.** con ghee-*ah*-cho
… with water.	**con acqua.** con *ah*-quah
… with soda.	**con seltz.** con selts
A gin …	**Un gin…** oon jeen
… and tonic.	**con tonico.** con *to*-nee-co
… with lemon.	**con limone.** con lee-*mo*-neh
A brandy.	**Un cognac.** oon con-*yahc*

Other essential expressions are the following.

Miss! [*This does not sound abrupt in Italian.*]	**Signorina!** seenyo-*ree*-nah
Waiter!	**Cameriere!** cameree-*air*-eh
The check, please.	**Il conto, per favore.** il *con*-to pair fa-*vo*-reh

How much does that come to?	**Quanto fa?** *quan*·to fah
Is the tip included?	**Il servizio è compreso?** il sair·*vit*·seeo eh com·*prai*·zo
Where is the restroom, please?	**Dov'è il bagno, per favore?** do·*veh* il *bahn*·yo pair fa·*vo*·reh

Ordering a Snack

Essential Information

- Look for cafés or bars with the following signs.

Birreria	Hot snacks	**Pizzeria**	Pizzeria
Panini/Tramezzini	Sandwiches	**Tavola calda**	Hot snacks
Pizze	Pizza	**Toasts**	Hot snacks

- In some regions, mobile vans sell hot snacks.

- In bars, if you want to eat your snack at the counter, you first pay at the cash register, then hand the receipt to the waiter behind the bar.

- For cakes, see p. 48.
  For ice cream, see p. 49.
  For picnic food, see p. 54.
  For ordering a drink, see p. 66.

- Small sandwiches called **tramezzini** are popular snacks and are made with a variety of fillings. Point to the one(s) you want.

- If olives, anchovies, potato chips, and nuts are available in bars, their price is normally included in the price of the drinks.

What to Say

I'll have …, please.	**Prendo, per favore,…** *pren*·do pair fa·*vo*·reh
… a cheese sandwich …	**un panino al formaggio.** oon pah·*nee*·no al for·*mahd*·jo
… a ham sandwich …	**un panino al prosciutto.** oon pah·*nee*·no al pro·*shoot*·to
… a salami sandwich …	**un panino al salame.** oon pah·*nee*·no al sa·*lah*·meh
… a sandwich (like that) …	**un tramezzino (così).** oon tramed·*zee*·no (co·*zee*)
… a pizza …	**una pizza.** *oo*·na *peet*·sah

Here are some other snacks you may want to try.

a small tomato pizza, usually eaten cold	**una pizzetta al pomodoro** *oo*·na peet·*set*·tah al pomo·*do*·ro
a savory bread, similar to pizza but without tomato sauce	**una focaccia** *oo*·na fo·*cah*·chah
a ham sandwich made with focaccia bread	**una focaccina al prosciutto** *oo*·na foca·*chee*·nah al pro·*shoot*·to
a toasted sandwich, normally made with ham and cheese	**un toast (al prosciutto e formaggio)** oon tost (al pro·*shoot*·to eh for·*mahd*·jo)

For other essential expressions, see "Ordering a Drink," p. 66.

In a Restaurant

Essential Information

· The place to ask for is **un ristorante** (see p. 11).

· You can eat at any of the following places.

Albergo	Hotel (*often with a fixed menu*)
Pensione	*Mainly for residents (fixed menu)*
Ristorante	
Trattoria	*Cheaper than a* **ristorante**

· Menus are always displayed outside larger restaurants; this is the *only* way to judge if a place suits you before entering.

· Some smaller restaurants do not have a printed or posted menu, and you must ask the waiter what is available.

· Self-service restaurants are rare.

· Service (15% to 20%) is always included in the bill, but an extra tip is usually welcome.

· Restaurants are legally required to give receipts, and you should insist on this.

· In southern Italy, the afternoon break is longer and dinner is eaten later in the evening than in the north.

What to Say

May I reserve a table?	**Potrei prenotare un tavolo?** po·*tray* preno·*tah*·reh oon *tah*·volo

I have reserved a table.	**Ho prenotato un tavolo.** o preno·*tah*·to oon *tah*·volo
A table …	**Un tavolo…** oon *tah*·volo
… for one.	**per una persona.** pair *oo*·na pair·*so*·nah
… for three.	**per tre persone.** pair treh pair·*so*·neh
The à la carte menu, please.	**Il menù alla carta, per favore.** il meh·*noo al*·la *car*·tah pair fa·*vo*·reh
The fixed price menu.	**Il menu a prezzo fisso.** il meh·*noo* ah *preht*·so *fis*·so
The tourist menu.	**Il menu turistico.** il meh·*noo* too·*ris*·tico
Today's special menu.	**I piatti del giorno.** ee pee·*aht*·tee del *jor*·no
What is this, please? [*point to an item on the menu*]	**Che cos'è questo, per favore?** keh co·*zeh ques*·to pair fa·*vo*·reh
A carafe of wine, please.	**Una caraffa di vino, per favore.** *oo*·na ca·*rahf*·fah dee *vee*·no pair fa·*vo*·reh
A quarter liter (250 cc).	**Un quarto.** oon *quar*·to
A half liter (500 cc).	**Un mezzo litro.** oon *med*·zo *lee*·tro
A liter.	**Un litro.** oon *lee*·tro
A glass.	**Un bicchiere.** oon beekee·*air*·eh
A bottle.	**Una bottiglia.** *oo*·na bot·*teel*·yah
A half-bottle.	**Una mezza bottiglia.** *oo*·na *med*·za bot·*teel*·yah
Red/white/rosé/house wine.	**Vino rosso/bianco/rosé/della casa.** *vee*·no *ros*·so/bee·*ahn*·co/ro·*zeh*/ *del*·la *cah*·sah
Some more bread, please.	**Ancora del pane, per favore.** an·*co*·rah del *pah*·neh pair fa·*vo*·reh
Some more wine.	**Ancora del vino.** an·*co*·rah del *vee*·no
Some oil.	**Dell'olio.** del·*lol*·yo

Some vinegar.	**Dell'aceto.**
	della·*cheh*·to
Some salt.	**Del sale.**
	del *sah*·leh
Some pepper.	**Del pepe.**
	del *peh*·peh
Some water.	**Dell'acqua.**
	del·*lah*·quah
Miss! [*This does not sound abrupt in Italian.*]	**Signorina!**
	seenyo·*ree*·nah
Waiter!	**Cameriere!**
	cameree·*air*·eh
The check, please.	**Il conto, per favore.**
	il *con*·to pair fa·*vo*·reh
How much does that come to?	**Quanto fa?**
	quan·to fah
Is the tip included?	**Il servizio è compreso?**
	il sair·*vit*·seeo eh com·*prai*·zo
Where is the restroom, please?	**Dov'è il bagno, per favore?**
	do·*veh* il *bahn*·yo pair fa·*vo*·reh
May I have a receipt?	**Potrei avere una ricevuta?**
	po·*tray* a·*vair*·eh *oo*·na riche·*voo*·tah

Here are some key words for meal courses, as seen on many menus.

What do you have in the way of …	**Che cosa avete come…**
	keh *co*·sah a·*veh*·teh *co*·meh
… appetizers?	**antipasti?**
	anti·*pahs*·tee
… cheese?	**formaggi?**
	for·*mahd*·jee
… dessert?	**dolci?**
	dol·chee
… egg dishes?	**uova?**
	wo·vah
… fish?	**pesce?**
	peh·sheh
… fowl?	**pollame?**
	pol·*lah*·meh
… fruit?	**frutta?**
	froot·tah
… game?	**selvaggina?**
	selvahd·*jee*·nah

What do you have in the way of …	**Che cosa avete come…** keh *co*·sah a·*veh*·teh *co*·meh
… ice cream?	**gelati?** je·*lah*·tee
… meat?	**carne?** *car*·neh
… soups?	**minestre?** mi·*nes*·treh
… vegetables?	**contorno?** con·*tor*·no

Pasta is part of the **minestre** course. See p. 77.

Understanding the Menu

Essential Information

- The main ingredients of most dishes are given on the following pages.

Appetizers (p. 54)	Fruit (p. 57)
Meat (p. 60)	Cheese (p. 52)
Fish (p. 63)	Ice cream (p. 49)
Vegetables (p. 57)	Dessert (p. 48)

  Together with the following list of cooking and menu terms, the ingredient and pasta lists should help you decode a menu.

- Dishes vary considerably from region to region in Italy: a dish with the same name, for example, **gnocchi alla romana** (dumplings Roman style), might be prepared differently in Rome and Milan—or even in two restaurants in the same city. Also, the same dish might appear on menus all over Italy with a different name in each region. If in doubt, ask the waiter.

- These cooking and menu terms are given for recognition only; for this reason, no pronunciation guide is given.

Cooking and Menu Terms

affumicato	smoked
all'aglio e olio	with garlic and oil
agrodolce	sweet-sour
arrosto	roast(ed)
al basilico	with basil
ben cotto	well done

con besciamella	with béchamel sauce
in bianco	boiled (not in a sauce)
bollito	boiled/stewed
alla bolognese	bolognese sauce
brasato	cooked in wine
al burro	cooked in butter
alla cacciatora	cooked in tomato sauce
al cartoccio	wrapped in foil and baked
alla casalinga	home style
al civet	marinated and cooked in wine
cotto	cooked (*as opposed to* raw)
crudo	raw
al dente	not overcooked, with a firm texture
dorato	slightly fried (golden)
alle erbe	with herbs
da farsi	to be prepared
ai ferri	grilled without oil
alla fiorentina	Florentine style
alla fonduta	with fondue
al forno	baked
fritto	fried
in gelatina	in savory jelly
grattugiato	grated and baked in cheese sauce
alla griglia	grilled over a fire
imbottiti	stuffed
lesso	boiled
in maionese	in/with mayonnaise
alle mandorle	with almonds
alla marinara	with seafood
al marsala	with Marsala wine
alla milanese	fried in egg and breadcrumbs
alla napoletana	Neapolitan style
all'origano	with oregano
in padella	cooked and served in a frying pan
al pangrattato	with breadcrumbs
alla panna	cooked in cream
al parmigiano	with parmesan cheese
al pecorino	with pecorino cheese
al pesto	with basil and garlic sauce
alla pizzaiola	with tomato sauce and cheese

al prezzemolo	with parsley
ragù	rich tomato and meat sauce for pasta
alla ricotta	with ricotta cheese
ripieno	stuffed
alla romana	Roman style
al rosmarino	with rosemary
in salmì	cooked in oil, vinegar, and herbs
salsa	sauce
salsa verde	parsley and garlic sauce
al sangue	cooked rare (*steak, etc.*)
alla siciliana	Sicilian style
spiedini	skewers
allo spiedo	on the spit
stufato	stew
al sugo	cooked in sauce
trifolato	cooked with tomato and parsley
in umido	steamed; stewed
alla veneziana	Venetian style
alle vongole	with clam (shellfish) sauce
allo zabaglione	with eggs, sugar, and Marsala sauce
zuppa	soup

Ingredients on Menus

abbacchio	young, spring lamb
amaretti	macaroons
anguilla	eel
animelle	sweetbreads
anitra	duck
baccalà	dried cod
bagna cauda	raw vegetables dipped in a sauce of hot oil, garlic, anchovies, and cream
bistecca alla fiorentina	T-bone steak
braciole	chops
brodo	broth
budino	*similar to* crème caramel; pudding
cacciagione	game
capperi	capers
capretto	kid
capriolo	deer

cassata	ice-cream cake with dried fruit
cervella	brains
cinghiale	boar
coppa	very lean bacon; cup (of ice cream)
costate	large chops
costolette	small chops, cutlets
cotechino	large pork sausage
crema	custard cream; cream soup
crostata	fruit or jam tart
crostini	small pieces of fried bread
fagiano	pheasant
fagioli	fresh or dried beans
fave	broad or butter beans
fegatini	chicken livers
fettine	small tender steaks
filetti	fillets
fragole di bosco	wild strawberries
frittata	omelet
frittelle	fritters
fritto misto	mixed fried meats
fritto di pesce	mixed fried fish
frutti di mare	shellfish
gelati	ice cream
granita	water ice
grissini	crispy bread sticks
involtini	slices of meat, stuffed and rolled
lepre	hare
limone	lemon
lombata	sirloin
macedonia	fruit salad
mandorle	almonds
minestrone	vegetable soup
mortadella	large mild salami similar to bologna
ossibuchi	dish of shin of veal
pancetta	bacon
panna	whipping cream
pasta asciutta	*generic term for* cooked pasta
pasta frolla	rich shortcake pastry
pasta sfogliata	puff pastry
peperonata	stew of green and red peppers

peperoncini	chili peppers
pernice	partridge
petti di pollo/tacchino	chicken/turkey breasts
piccata	small veal slices
pignoli	pine nuts
pinzimonio	raw vegetables to dip in oil
pizza	flat "bread" spread with tomato sauce
polpette	meatballs
prosciutto di Parma	raw ham from Parma
quaglia	quail
riso	rice
risotto	rice cooked in sauce
rollata	meat loaf stuffed with herbs
salame all'aglio	garlic sauce
salsiccia	sausage
saltimbocca alla romana	fried veal with ham and rosemary
scaloppine	small veal slices
semifreddo	ice cream with a biscuit
seppie	cuttlefish
spezzatino	stew
stracciatella	hot broth with beaten eggs
stracotto	beef stew with vegetables
tacchino	turkey
tartufi	truffles
torta	cake
trippa	tripe
uccelli	small birds (*for example,* thrushes)
uova	eggs
vongole	clams
zampone	pig's foot stuffed with chopped, seasoned meat
zuppa inglese	chocolate trifle
zuppa pavese	broth, lightly boiled egg and cheese

Types of Pasta

agnolini/agnolotti	similar to ravioli
cannelloni	large tubular pasta, often stuffed
cappelletti	stuffed pasta rings
conchiglie	shell-shaped pasta

ditali	short tubular pasta
farfalle	butterfly-shaped pasta
fettuccine	narrow ribbons of pasta
gnocchi	small potato or semolina "dumplings"
lasagne	wide flat pasta
maccheroni	large hollow spaghetti
pasta asciutta	*generic term for* cooked pasta
pasta in brodo	small shapes of pasta in broth
polenta	porridge of maize flour
ravioli	stuffed square-shaped pasta
rigatoni	large-grooved tubular pasta
spaghetti	long, thin, round pasta
tagliatelle	narrow ribbon pasta
tortellini	stuffed pasta rings
vermicelli	very thin spaghetti; "little worms"
ziti	tubular-shaped pasta

Health

Essential Information

- For details of reciprocal health agreements between your country and the country you are visiting, visit your local Department of Health office at least one month before leaving, or ask your travel agent.

- It is a good idea to purchase a medical insurance policy through a travel agent, an insurance broker, or a travel organization.

- The Italian state medical insurance is called **INAM**.

- Take an "emergency" first-aid kit with you.

- For minor health problems and treatment at a drugstore, see p. 30.

- For asking the way to a doctor, dentist, drugstore, or Health and Social Security Office (for reimbursement), see p. 10.

- Once in Italy, determine a plan of action in case of serious illness: communicate your problem to a neighbor, the receptionist, or someone you see regularly. You are then dependent on that person to help you obtain treatment.

- To find a doctor in an emergency, look for **Medici** in the Yellow Pages of the telephone directory. Here are important signs to look for.

Ambulatorio	Doctor's office
H	Hospital
Ospedale	Hospital
Pronto soccorso	Emergency room; first aid

- Dial 113 for emergency ambulance service.

What Is the Matter?

I have a pain in my …	**Mi fa male…** mee fah *mah*·leh
… ankle.	**la caviglia.** la ca·*veel*·yah
… arm.	**il braccio.** il *brah*·cho
… back.	**la schiena.** la skee·*eh*·nah
… bladder.	**la vescica.** la veh·*shee*·cah
… bowels.	**l'intestino.** lintes·*tee*·no

I have a pain in my …	**Mi fa male…** mee fah *mah*·leh
… breast.	**il seno.** il *seh*·no
… chest.	**il torace.** il to·*rah*·cheh
… ear.	**l'orecchio.** lo·*reh*·keeo
… eye.	**l'occhio.** *lo*·keeo
… foot.	**il piede.** il pee·*eh*·deh
… head.	**la testa.** la *tes*·tah
… heel.	**il calcagno.** il cahl·*cahn*·yo
… jaw.	**la mandibola.** la man·*dee*·bolah
… kidney.	**il rene.** il *reh*·neh
… leg.	**la gamba.** la *gahm*·bah
… lung.	**il polmone.** il pol·*mo*·neh
… neck.	**il collo.** il *col*·lo
… penis.	**il pene.** il *peh*·neh
… shoulder.	**la spalla.** la *spahl*·lah
… stomach (abdomen).	**lo stomaco (addome).** lo *sto*·maco (ad·*do*·meh)
… testicle.	**il testicolo.** il tes·*tee*·colo
… throat.	**la gola.** la *go*·lah
… vagina.	**la vagina.** la vah·*jee*·nah
… wrist.	**il polso.** il *pol*·so
I have a pain here. [*point*]	**Ho un dolore qui.** o oon do·*lo*·reh quee

I have a toothache.	**Ho male a un dente.** o *mah*·leh ah oon *den*·teh
I have broken …	**Ho rotto…** o *rot*·to
… my dentures.	**la dentiera.** la dentee·*air*·ah
… my glasses.	**gli occhiali.** l·yee okee·*ah*·lee
I have lost …	**Ho perso…** o *pair*·so
… my contact lenses.	**le lenti a contatto.** leh *len*·tee ah con·*taht*·to
… a filling.	**un'otturazione.** oonottoorahtsee·*o*·neh
My son is ill.	**Mio figlio è ammalato.** *mee*·o *feel*·yo eh amma·*lah*·to
My daughter is ill.	**Mia figlia è ammalata.** *mee*·ah *feel*·yah eh amma·*lah*·tah
He/she has a pain in his/her …	**Ha un dolore…** ah oon do·*lo*·reh
… ankle. [*see list above*]	**alla caviglia.** *al*·la ca·*veel*·yah
… arm. [*see list above*]	**al braccio.** al *brah*·cho

How Bad Is It?

I am ill.	**Sto male.** sto *mah*·leh
It is urgent.	**È urgente.** eh oor·*jen*·teh
It is serious.	**È grave.** eh *grah*·veh
It is not serious.	**Non è grave.** non eh *grah*·veh
It hurts.	**Fa male.** fah *mah*·leh
It hurts a lot.	**Fa molto male.** fah *mol*·to *mah*·leh
It doesn't hurt a lot.	**Non fa troppo male.** non fah *trop*·po *mah*·leh
The pain occurs …	**Il dolore si ripete…** il do·*lo*·reh see ree·*pet*·teh
… every quarter of an hour.	**ogni quarto d'ora.** *on*·yee *quar*·to *do*·rah

The pain occurs …	**Il dolore si ripete…** il do·*lo*·reh see ree·*pet*·teh
… every half hour.	**ogni mezz'ora.** *on*·yee med·*zo*·rah
… every hour.	**ogni ora.** *on*·yee *o*·rah
… every day.	**ogni giorno.** *on*·yee *jor*·no
… most of the time.	**quasi sempre.** *quah*·zee *sem*·preh
I've had it for …	**L'ho da…** lo da
… one hour/one day.	**un'ora/un giorno.** oo·*no*·rah/oon *jor*·no
… two hours/two days.	**due ore/due giorni.** *doo*·eh *o*·reh/*doo*·eh *jor*·nee
It is a …	**È…** eh
… sharp pain.	**un dolore acuto.** oon do·*lo*·reh a·*coo*·to
… dull ache.	**un dolore sordo.** oon do·*lo*·reh *sor*·do
… nagging pain.	**un dolore continuo.** oon do·*lo*·reh con·*tee*·noo·o
I feel …	**Mi sento…** mee *sen*·to
… weak.	**debole.** *deh*·bo·leh
… feverish.	**la febbre.** la *feb*·breh

Are you already being treated for something else?

I take … regularly. [*show medication*]	**Prendo regolarmente…** *pren*·do regolar·*men*·teh
… this medicine …	**questa medicina.** *ques*·tah medi·*chee*·nah
… these pills …	**queste pillole.** *ques*·teh *peel*·loleh
I have …	**Ho…** o
… a heart condition.	**mal di cuore.** mahl dee *kwo*·reh
… hemorrhoids.	**le emorroidi.** leh eh·mor·*roy*·dee

I have …	**Ho…**
	o
… rheumatism.	**i reumatismi.**
	ee reh·ooma·*tees*·mee
I am …	**Sono…**
	so·no
… allergic to (penicillin).	**allergico** (*male*)/**allergica** (*female*)
	alla (penicillina).
	al·*lair*·jeeco/al·*lair*·jeecah
	al·la (penichil·*lee*·nah).
… asthmatic.	**asmatico** (*male*)/**asmatica** (*female*).
	ahz·*mah*·teeco/ahz·*mah*·teecah
… diabetic.	**diabetico** (*male*)/**diabetica** (*female*).
	deeah·*beh*·teeco/deeah·*beh*·teecah
… pregnant.	**incinta.**
	een·*cheen*·tah

Other Essential Expressions

Please, can you help?	**Mi può aiutare, per favore?**
	mee poo·*o* ahyoo·*tah*·reh pair
	fa·*vo*·reh
A doctor, please.	**Un dottore, per favore.**
	oon dot·*to*·reh pair fa·*vo*·reh
A dentist.	**Un dentista.**
	oon den·*tees*·tah
I don't speak Italian.	**Non parlo italiano.**
	non *par*·lo italee·*ah*·no
(At) what time does … arrive?	**A che ora arriva…**
	ah keh orah ar·*ree*·vah
… the dentist …	**il dentista?**
	il den·*tees*·tah
… the doctor …	**il dottore?**
	il dot·*to*·reh

Here are important things the doctor may tell you.

Take this …	**Prenda questo…**
	pren·dah *ques*·to
… every day/hour.	**ogni giorno/ora.**
	on·yee *jor*·no/*o*·rah
… twice/four times a day.	**due/quattro volte al giorno.**
	doo·eh/*quaht*·tro *vol*·teh al *jor*·no
Stay in bed.	**Stia a letto.**
	stee·ah ah *let*·to

Don't travel for _____ days/weeks.

Non viaggi per _____ giorni/settimane.
non vee·*ahd*·jee pair …
jor·nee/setti·*mah*·neh

You must go to the hospital.

Deve andare in ospedale.
deh·veh an·*dah*·reh in
ospeh·*dah*·leh

Problems:
Complaints, Loss, and Theft

Essential Information

- If you have problems with …
    … camping facilities, see p. 21.
    … household appliances, see p. 41.
    … your health, see p. 79.
    … a car, see p. 94.

- If worse comes to worst, go to the police station. To ask directions, see p. 9.

- Look for the following signs.

Carabinieri/Polizia	Police
Questura	Police station
Vigili urbani	Traffic cops

- If you lose your passport, go to your nearest Consulate.

- In an emergency, dial 113 for fire and police.

Complaints

I bought this …	**Ho comprato questo…** o com·*prah*·to *ques*·to
… today.	**oggi.** *od*·jee
… yesterday.	**ieri.** *yeh*·ree
… on Monday.	**lunedì.** looneh·*dee*

For days of the week, see p. 117.

It is defective.	**Non va bene.** non va *ben*·eh
Look.	**Guardi.** *guar*·dee
Here. [*point*]	**Qui.** quee

Can you …	**Potrebbe…** po·*treb*·beh
… exchange it?	**cambiarlo?** cambee·*ar*·lo
… repair it?	**aggiustarlo?** adjoo·*star*·lo
Here is the receipt.	**Ecco la ricevuta.** *ec*·co la riche·*voo*·tah
Can I have a refund?	**Mi può rimborsare?** mee poo·*o* rimbor·*sah*·reh
Can I see the manager?	**Posso vedere il direttore?** *pos*·so veh·*dair*·eh il diret·*to*·reh

Loss

See also "Theft" below. The lists are interchangeable.

I have lost …	**Ho perso…** o *pair*·so
… my bracelet.	**il braccialetto.** il brahcha·*let*·to
… my camera.	**la macchina fotografica.** la *mah*·keenah foto·*grah*·feecah
… my car keys.	**le chiavi della macchina.** leh kee·*ah*·vee *del*·la *mah*·keenah
… my car registration.	**il libretto della macchina.** il lee·*bret*·to *del*·la *mah*·keenah
… my driver's license.	**la patente.** la pa·*ten*·teh
… my insurance certificate.	**il certificato dell'assicurazione.** il chairteefee·*cah*·to dellasseecoorahtsee·*o*·neh
… my jewelry.	**i gioielli.** ee joy·*el*·lee
… my purse/handbag.	**la borsa.** la *bor*·sah
… everything!	**tutto!** *toot*·to

Theft

See also "Loss" above; the lists are interchangeable.

Someone has stolen …	**Qualcuno mi ha rubato…**
	qual·*coo*·no mee ah roo·*bah*·to
… my car.	**la macchina.**
	la *mah*·keenah
… my car radio.	**la radio della macchina.**
	la *rah*·deeo *del*·la *mah*·keenah
… my keys.	**le chiavi.**
	leh kee·*ah*·vee
… my luggage.	**i bagagli.**
	ee ba·*gahl*·yee
… my money.	**i soldi.**
	ee *sol*·dee
… my necklace.	**la collana.**
	la col·*lah*·nah
… my passport.	**il passaporto.**
	il passa·*por*·to
… my radio.	**la radio.**
	la *rah*·deeo
… my tickets.	**i biglietti.**
	ee beel·*yet*·tee
… my traveler's checks.	**i traveler's checks.**
	ee *tra*·vellerz checks
… my wallet.	**il portafoglio.**
	il porta·*fol*·yo
… my watch.	**l'orologio.**
	loro·*lod*·jo

Likely Reactions

Wait.	**Aspetti.**
	as·*pet*·tee
When?	**Quando?**
	quan·do
Where?	**Dove?**
	do·veh
Your name?	**Il suo nome?**
	il *soo*·o *no*·meh
Address?	**L'indirizzo?**
	lindi·*reet*·so
I can't help you.	**Non posso aiutarla.**
	non *pos*·so ahyoo·*tar*·lah
I can't do anything about it.	**Non posso farci nulla.**
	non *pos*·so *far*·chee *nool*·lah

The Post Office

Essential Information

- For finding a post office, see p. 9.
- Here are signs to look for.

  Posta
  Poste e Telegrafi (P.T.)
  Poste e Telecomunicazioni (PP.TT.)

- It is best to buy stamps at a tobacco shop. Only go to the post office for more complicated transactions, such as sending a telegram. For signs indicating tobacco shops, see p. 35.
- Mailboxes are usually red.
- To have your mail "held," show your passport at the counter marked **Fermo Posta** in the main post office; you will pay a small charge.

What to Say

To the United States, please. [*hand letters, cards, or parcels over the counter*]	**Per gli Stati Uniti, per favore.** pair l·yee *stah*·tee oo·*nee*·tee pair fa·*vo*·reh
To Australia.	**Per l'Australia.** pair lah·oo·*strahl*·yah

For names of countries, see p. 121.

How much is …	**Quanto costa spedire…** *quan*·to *cos*·ta speh·*dee*·reh
… this parcel (to Canada)?	**questo pacco (in Canada)?** *ques*·to *pac*·co (in *cah*·nadah)
… a letter (to Australia)?	**una lettera (in Australia)?** *oo*·na *let*·terah (in ah·oo·*strahl*·yah)
… a postcard (to the United States)?	**una cartolina (negli Stati Uniti)?** *oo*·na carto·*lee*·nah (*nel*·yee *stah*·tee oo·*nee*·tee)
Air mail.	**Via aerea.** *vee*·ah ah·*air*·eh·ah
Surface mail.	**Via normale.** *vee*·ah nor·*mah*·leh
One stamp, please.	**Un francobollo, per favore.** oon franco·*bol*·lo pair fa·*vo*·reh
Two stamps.	**Due francobolli.** *doo*·eh franco·*bol*·lee

A one-euro stamp.	**Un francobollo da un euro.**
	oon franco·*bol*·lo da oon *eh*·oo·ro
I would like to send a telegram.	**Vorrei spedire un telegramma.**
	vor·*ray* speh·*dee*·reh oon
	tele·*grahm*·mah

Telephoning

Essential Information

- Unless you read and speak Italian well, it is best not to make telephone calls by yourself. Go to the main post office and write the town and number you want to call on a sheet of paper. Add **con preavviso** if you want to place a person-to-person call, or **spese a carico del ricevente** if you want to reverse the charges.

- Telephone booths are gray or red. Public telephones are found in most bars.

- To ask directions to a public telephone, see p. 12.

- To use a public telephone, you buy a special card (**una scheda telefonica,** sold in bars, tobacco shops, telephone centers, and newsstands) or use coins. For local calls (**chiamate urbane**), insert coins or the **scheda telefonica** and wait for the dial tone before dialing the number. For long-distance calls (**chiamate interurbane**), use coins or the **scheda telefonica**.

- To call the United States, dial the country code 1, then the area code and number you want to call.

- If you use an international calling card, dial the access number on the back of the card. You will be prompted to dial the PIN number for the card, then the number you want to reach.

- The international calling card is the most convenient and least expensive way to make an international call. You can purchase it at telephone centers, which are found everywhere in Italy.

What to Say

Where can I make a telephone call?	**Dove posso fare una telefonata?** *do·*veh *pos·*so *fah·*reh *oo·*na telefo·*nah·*tah
Local call.	**Telefonata urbana.** telefo·*nah·*tah oor·*bah·*nah
Long-distance call. (*within Italy*)	**Telefonata interurbana.** telefo·*nah·*tah intairoor·*bah·*nah
Long-distance call. (*international*)	**Telefonata internazionale.** telefo·*nah·*tah intairnahtsee·o·*nah·*leh

I would like this number … [*show number*]	**Vorrei questo numero…** vor·*ray* ques·to *noo*·mero
… in Canada.	**in Canada.** in *cah*·nadah
… in the United States.	**negli Stati Uniti.** *nel*·yee stah·tee oo·nee·tee

For the names of other countries, see p. 121.

Can you dial it for me, please?	**Può farmi il numero, per favore?** poo·*o far*·mee il *noo*·mero pair fa·*vo*·reh
How much is it?	**Quanto Le devo?** *quan*·to leh *deh*·vo
Hello!	**Pronto!** *pron*·to
May I speak to _____ ?	**Posso parlare con _____ .** *pos*·so par·*lah*·reh con…
Extension _____ .	**Interno _____ .** in·*tair*·no…
I'm sorry; I don't speak Italian.	**Mi dispiace, non parlo italiano.** mee deespee·*ah*·cheh non *par*·lo italee·*ah*·no
Do you speak English?	**Parla inglese?** *par*·lah in·*glai*·zeh
Thank you, I'll call back.	**Grazie, ritelefonerò.** *graht*·see·eh ritelefone·*ro*
Good-bye.	**Arrivederci.** areeve·*dair*·chee

Likely Reactions

That is one and a half euros.	**Fa un euro e cinquanta.** fah oon *eh*·oo·ro eh chin·*quan*·tah
Booth number (3).	**Cabina numero (3).** ca·*bee*·nah *noo*·mero (treh)
Don't hang up.	**Attenda.** at·*ten*·dah
I am trying to connect you.	**Cerco di collegarla.** *chair*·co dee colle·*gar*·lah
You are connected.	**Parli pure.** *par*·lee *poo*·reh
There is a delay.	**C'è un ritardo.** cheh oon ree·*tar*·do
I'll try again.	**Proverò ancora.** prove·*ro* an·*co*·rah

Cashing Checks and Changing Money

Essential Information

- To ask directions to a bank or currency exchange office, see p. 10.
- Look for the following words to find banking facilities.

Banca/Banco	Bank
Cambio valute	Currency exchange
Istituto bancario	Bank

- Personal checks from United States banks are not accepted or exchanged in Italy.
- To get cash, use ATM (Bancomat) machines, which are located outside all banks.
- To cash traveler's checks, go to a bank or currency exchange office. Have your passport handy.

What to Say

I would like to cash …
> **Vorrei incassare…**
> vor·*ray* incas·*sah*·reh

… this traveler's check.
> **questo traveler's check.**
> *ques*·to *tra*·velerz check

… these traveler's checks.
> **questi traveler's checks.**
> *ques*·tee *tra*·velerz checks

I would like to change this into euros.
> **Vorrei cambiare questi soldi in euro.**
> vor·*ray* cambee·*ah*·reh *ques*·tee
> *sol*·dee in *eh*·oo·ro

Here is …
> **Ecco…**
> *ec*·co

… my ATM card.
> **la mia carta assegni.**
> la *mee*·ah *car*·tah as·*sen*·yee

… my passport.
> **il mio passaporto.**
> il *mee*·o passa·*por*·to

To exchange currency for excursions into neighboring countries, use the following expressions.

I would like to exchange this ... [show banknotes]	**Vorrei cambiare questi soldi...** vor·*ray* cambee·*ah*·reh *ques*·tee *sol*·dee
... into Swiss francs.	**in franchi svizzeri.** in *frahn*·kee *zveet*·seree
... into British pounds.	**in sterline inglesi.** in ster·*lee*·neh in·*glai*·zee
What is the exchange rate today?	**Qual'è il cambio oggi?** quah·*leh* il *cahm*·beeo *od*·jee

Likely Reactions

Passport, please.	**Il passaporto, per favore.** il passa·*por*·to pair fa·*vo*·reh
Sign here.	**Firmi qui.** *feer*·mee quee
Your ATM card, please.	**La sua carta assegni, per favore.** la *soo*·ah *car*·tah as·*sen*·yee pair fa·*vo*·reh
Go to the cashier's window.	**Si accomodi alla cassa.** see ac·*co*·modee *al*·la *cahs*·sah

Automobile Travel

Essential Information

- To ask directions to a gas station or garage, see p. 11.
- Is it a self-service station? Look for the sign **Self-service**.
- There are three grades of gasoline.

Benzina senza piombo	Regular lead-free
Benzina super senza piombo	Premium lead-free
Gasolio diesel	Diesel

- One gallon is the equivalent of 3.785 liters.
- Gasoline stations are usually closed between 12 noon and 3 P.M., and very few offer 24-hour service (except on highways).
- For car repairs, look for the following signs.

Autoriparazioni	Repairs
Autorimessa	Garage
Carrozzeria	Bodywork
Elettrauto	Car electrician
Meccanico	Mechanic

- In case of a breakdown or an emergency, look for an **ACI** (Italian Automobile Club) sign, or dial 116 from a public telephone.
- For road signs and warnings, see p. 109.

What to Say

For numbers, see p. 113.

(Nine) liters of …	**(Nove) litri di…**
	(*no*·veh) *lee*·tree dee
(Ten) euros of …	**(Dieci) euro di…**
	(dee·*eh*·chee) *eh*·oo·ro dee
… regular/premium/diesel.	**senza piombo/super/gasolio.**
	saint·sah pee·*om*·bo/*soo*·per/
	ga·*zol*·yo
Fill it up, please.	**Pieno, per favore.**
	pee·*eh*·no pair fa·*vo*·reh
Will you check …	**Può controllare…**
	poo·*o* control·*lah*·reh
… the battery?	**la batteria?**
	la batte·*ree*·ah

Will you check …	**Può controllare…**
	poo·*o* control·*lah*·reh
… the oil?	**l'olio?**
	lol·yo
… the radiator?	**il radiatore?**
	il radeeah·*to*·reh
… the tires?	**le gomme?**
	leh *gom*·meh
I have run out of gasoline.	**Sono rimasta senza benzina.**
	so·no ree·*mahs*·tah *saint*·sah
	ben·*zee*·nah
Can I borrow a can, please?	**Posso prendere in prestito una latta, per favore?**
	pos·so *pren*·dereh in *pres*·teeto
	oo·na *laht*·tah pair fa·*vo*·reh
My car has broken down.	**La mia macchina s'è rotta.**
	la *mee*·ah *mah*·keenah seh *rot*·tah
My car won't start.	**La mia macchina non parte.**
	la *mee*·ah *mah*·keenah non *par*·teh
I have had an accident.	**Ho avuto un incidente.**
	o a·*voo*·to oon inchee·*den*·teh
I have lost my car keys.	**Ho perso le chiavi della macchina.**
	o *pair*·so leh kee·*ah*·vee *del*·la
	mah·keenah
My car is …	**La mia macchina è…**
	la *mee*·ah *mah*·keenah eh
… two kilometers away.	**a due chilometri.**
	ah *doo*·eh kee·*lo*·metree
… three kilometers away.	**a tre chilometri.**
	ah treh kee·*lo*·metree
Can you help me, please?	**Mi può aiutare, per favore?**
	mee poo·*o* ahyoo·*tah*·reh pair
	fa·*vo*·reh
Do you repair cars?	**Ripara le macchine?**
	ree·*pah*·rah leh *mah*·keeneh
I have a flat tire.	**Ho una gomma a terra.**
	o *oo*·na *gom*·mah ah *ter*·rah
I have a broken windshield.	**Ho rotto il parabrezza.**
	o *rot*·to il para·*bret*·sah
I think the problem is here. [*point*]	**Penso che il guasto sia qui.**
	pen·so keh il *guahs*·to *see*·ah quee
I don't know what is wrong.	**Non so cosa non va.**
	non so *co*·sa non va

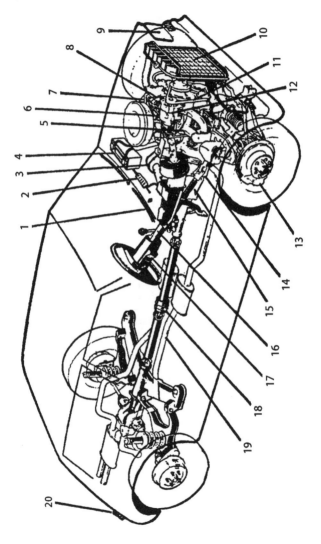

1	windshield wipers	**tergicristalli** tairjeecris-*tah*-lee	11	fan belt	**cinghia del ventilatore** *chin*-gheeah del ventila-*to*-reh
2	fuses	**fusibili** foo-*zee*-bilee	12	generator/alternator	**dinamo** *dee*-namo
3	heater	**riscaldamento** riscalda-*men*-to	13	brakes	**freni** *freh*-nee
4	battery	**batteria** batte-*ree*-ah	14	clutch	**frizione** freetsee-*o*-neh
5	engine	**motore** mo-*to*-reh	15	gear box	**cambio** *cahm*-beeo
6	fuel pump	**pompa benzina** *pom*-pah ben-*zee*-nah	16	steering	**sterzo** *stairt*-so
7	starter	**motorino d'avviamento** moto-*ree*-no davveeah-*men*-to	17	ignition	**accensione** achensee-*o*-neh
8	carburetor	**carburatore** carboora-*to*-reh	18	transmission	**trasmissione** trasmissee-*o*-neh
9	lights	**luci** *loo*-chee	19	exhaust	**scappamento** scappa-*men*-to
10	radiator	**radiatore** radeeah-*to*-reh	20	turn signals	**lampeggiatori** lampedja-*to*-ree

Can you …

Può…
poo·o

… repair the faulty part?

riparare il guasto?
reepa·rah·reh il guahs·to

… come and look?

venire a vedere?
ve·nee·reh ah veh·dair·eh

… give me an estimate?

farmi un preventivo?
far·mee oon preven·tee·vo

… write it down?

scriverlo?
scree·verlo

How long will it take to
repair it?

Quanto ci vorrà per ripararlo?
quan·to chee vor·rah pair
reepa·rar·lo

When will the car be ready?

Quando sarà pronta la macchina?
quan·do sa·rah pron·tah la
mah·keenah

Can I see the bill?

Posso vedere il conto?
pos·so veh·dair·eh il con·to

Renting a Car

Can I rent a car?

Potrei noleggiare una macchina?
po·tray noled·jah·reh oo·na
mah·keenah

I need a car …

Ho bisogno di una macchina…
o bee·son·yo dee oo·na mah·keenah

… for two people …

per due persone
pair doo·eh pair·so·neh

… for five people …

per cinque persone
pair chin·queh pair·so·neh

… for one day.

per un giorno.
pair oon jor·no

… for five days.

per cinque giorni.
pair chin·queh jor·nee

… for a week.

per una settimana.
pair oo·na setti·mah·nah

Can you write down …

Può scrivermi…
Poo·o scree·vermee

… the deposit to pay?

quant'è il deposito da pagare?
quan·teh il de·po·zeeto da
pa·gah·reh

… the charge per kilometer?

quanto costa al chilometro?
quan·to cos·tah al kee·lo·metro

… the daily charge?

quanto costa al giorno?
quan·to cos·tah al jor·no

Can you write down …	**Può scrivermi…**
	Poo·*o* scree·vermee
… the cost of insurance?	**il costo dell'assicurazione?**
	il *cos*·to dellassicoorahtsee·*o*·neh
Can I leave it in (Turin)?	**Posso lasciarla a (Torino)?**
	pos·so la·*shar*·lah ah (to·*ree*·no)
What documents do I need?	**Quali documenti ci vogliono?**
	quah·lee docoo·*men*·tee chee *vol*·yono

Likely Reactions

I don't do repairs.	**Non riparo auto.**
	non ree·*pah*·ro ah·*oo*·to
Where is your car?	**Dov'è la sua macchina?**
	do·*veh* la *soo*·ah *mah*·keenah
What make is it?	**Che tipo di macchina è?**
	keh *tee*·po dee *mah*·keenah eh
Come back tomorrow/ on Monday.	**Ritorni domani/lunedì.**
	ree·*tor*·nee do·*mah*·nee/looneh·*dee*

For days of the week, see p. 117.

We don't rent cars.	**Non noleggiamo macchine.**
	non noled·*jah*·mo *mah*·keeneh
Your driver's license, please.	**La patente, per favore.**
	la pa·*ten*·teh pair fa·*vo*·reh
The mileage is unlimited.	**Il chilometraggio è illimitato.**
	il keelome·*trahd*·jo eh illimi·*tah*·to

Public Transportation

Essential Information

- To ask directions to a bus stop, the bus station, the railway station, or a taxi stand, see p. 10.
- Standing in line for buses is unheard of in Italy.
- Taxis can be found at taxi stands in the main areas of town, especially at the railway station.
- Here are the different types of trains, listed according to speed (slowest to fastest).

  Locale
  Diretto
  Espresso
  Rapido

  Sometimes **Rapido** is first-class only; a supplement is charged and seats are reserved, especially on luxury high-speed trains.

- Here are the signs to look for. (See also p. 109.)

Biglietti	Tickets
Binario	Track/platform
Deposito bagagli	Luggage storage
Entrata	Entrance
Fermata autobus	Bus stop
Ferrovie dello Stato/F.S.	State Railways
Informazioni	Information
Orario	Timetable
Proibito/Vietato	Prohibited
Salita	Entrance (for buses and streetcars)
Uscita	Exit

- In the major cities, automatic ticket validation machines are in operation on buses, streetcars, and the subway. Tickets must be bought in advance from bars, tobacco shops, and magazine stands. Ask for details at the local tourist information office (see p. 14).

What to Say

Where does the train for (Rome) leave from?	**Da dove parte il treno per (Roma)?** da *do*·veh *par*·teh il *treh*·no pair (*ro*·mah)

(At) what time does the train leave for (Milan)?	**A che ora parte il treno per (Milano)?** ah keh *o*·rah *par*·teh il *treh*·no pair (mee·*lah*·no)
(At) what time does the train arrive in (Turin)?	**A che ora arriva il treno a (Torino)?** ah keh *o*·rah ar·*ree*·vah il *treh*·no ah (to·*ree*·no)
Is this the train for (Venice)?	**È questo il treno per (Venezia)?** eh *ques*·to il *treh*·no pair (veh·*net*·seeah)
Where does the bus for (Florence) leave from?	**Da dove parte l'autobus per (Firenze)?** da *do*·veh *par*·teh la·*oo*·toboos pair (fee·*rent*·seh)
(At) what time does the bus arrive in (Naples)?	**A che ora arriva l'autobus a (Napoli)?** ah keh *o*·rah ar·*ree*·vah la·*oo*·toboos ah (*nah*·polee)
Is this the bus for (Palermo)?	**È questo l'autobus per (Palermo)?** eh *ques*·to la·*oo*·toboos pair (pah·*lair*·mo)
Do I have to change?	**Devo cambiare?** *deh*·vo cambee·*ah*·reh
Where does … leave from?	**Da dove parte…** da *do*·veh *par*·teh
… the bus …	**l'autobus** la·*oo*·toboos
… the train …	**il treno** il *treh*·no
… the subway …	**la metropolitana** la metropoli·*tah*·nah
… the boat/ferry …	**il vaporetto/il traghetto** il vapo·*ret*·to/il trah·*ghet*·to
… for the airport?	**per l'aeroporto?** pair lah·airo·*por*·to
… for the cathedral?	**per la cattedrale?** pair la catte·*drah*·leh
… for the beach?	**per la spiaggia?** pair la spee·*ahd*·jah
… for the marketplace?	**per il mercato?** pair il mair·*cah*·to
… for the train station?	**per la stazione?** pair la stahtsee·*o*·neh

Where does … leave from?   **Da dove parte…**
                                   da *do*·veh *par*·teh

… the bus …   **l'autobus**
                                   la·*oo*·toboos

… the train …   **il treno**
                                   il *treh*·no

… the subway …   **la metropolitana**
                                   la metropoli·*tah*·nah

… the boat/ferry …   **il vaporetto/il traghetto**
                                   il vapo·*ret*·to/il trah·*ghet*·to

… for the center of town?   **per il centro città?**
                                   pair il *chen*·tro chit·*tah*

… for the town hall?   **per il municipio?**
                                   pair il mooni·*chee*·peeo

… for (St. John's) Church?   **per la chiesa (di S. Giovanni)?**
                                   pair la kee·*eh*·zah (dee sahn
                                   jo·*vah*·nee)

… for the swimming pool?   **per la piscina?**
                                   pair la pi·*shee*·nah

Is this …   **È questo…**
                                   eh *ques*·to

… the bus to the marketplace?   **l'autobus per il mercato?**
                                   la·*oo*·toboos pair il mair·*cah*·to

… the streetcar to the train   **il tram per la stazione?**
station?   il trahm pair la stahtsee·*o*·neh

Where can I get a taxi?   **Dove posso trovare un taxi?**
                                   do·veh *pos*·so tro·*vah*·reh oon *tah*·xi

Can you drop me off at the   **Può farmi scendere alla fermata**
right stop, please?   **giusta, per favore?**
                                   poo·*o far*·mee *shen*·dereh *al*·la
                                   fair·*mah*·tah *joo*·stah pair fa·*vo*·reh

Can I reserve a seat?   **Posso prenotare un posto?**
                                   pos·so preno·*tah*·reh oon *pos*·to

One way.   **Solo andata.**
                                   so·lo an·*dah*·tah

Round trip.   **Andata e ritorno.**
                                   an·*dah*·tah eh ree·*tor*·no

First class.   **Prima classe.**
                                   pree·mah *clahs*·seh

Second class.   **Seconda classe.**
                                   se·*con*·dah *clahs*·seh

One adult …	**Un adulto…** oon a·*dool*·to
Two adults …	**Due adulti…** *doo*·eh a·*dool*·tee
… and one child.	**e un bambino.** eh oon bam·*bee*·no
… and two children.	**e due bambini.** eh *doo*·eh bam·*bee*·nee
How much is it?	**Quanto costa?** *quan*·to *cos*·tah

Likely Reactions

Over there.	**Di là.** dee lah
Here.	**Qui.** quee
Track (1).	**Binario (uno).** bee·*nah*·reeo (*oo*·no)
At (four o'clock).	**Alle (quattro).** *al*·leh (*quaht*·tro)

For telling time, see p. 115.

Change in (Milan).	**Cambi a (Milano).** *cahm*·bee ah (mee·*lah*·no)
Change at (the town hall).	**Cambi al (municipio).** *cahm*·bee al (mooni·*chee*·peeo)
This is your stop.	**Questa è la sua fermata.** *ques*·tah eh la *soo*·ah fair·*mah*·tah
There is only first class.	**C'è solo la prima classe.** cheh *so*·lo la *pree*·mah *clahs*·seh
There is a supplement.	**C'è un supplemento.** cheh oon soopple·*men*·to

Leisure and Entertainment

Essential Information

- To ask directions to a place of entertainment, see p. 12.
  For telling time, see p. 115.
  For important signs, see p. 109.

- At the more popular seaside resorts, you pay to go to the beach and to rent lounge chairs and umbrellas.

- Smoking is forbidden in cinemas and theaters, unless otherwise specified.

- Theater ushers should be tipped.

What to Say

(At) what time does … open?	**A che ora apre…** ah keh *o*·rah *a*·preh
(At) what time does … close?	**A che ora chiude…** ah keh *o*·rah kee·*oo*·deh
… the art gallery …	**la galleria d'arte?** la galle·*ree*·ah *dar*·teh
… the botanical garden …	**il giardino botanico?** il jar·*dee*·no bo·*tah*·neeco
… the cinema …	**il cinema?** il *chee*·nemah
… the concert hall …	**l'auditorium?** lah·oodee·*to*·ree·oom
… the disco …	**la discoteca?** la disco·*tec*·cah
… the museum …	**il museo?** il moo·*zai*·o
… the nightclub …	**il night?** il night
… the sports stadium …	**lo stadio?** lo *stah*·deeo
… the swimming pool …	**la piscina?** la pi·*shee*·nah
… the theater …	**il teatro?** il teh·*ah*·tro
… the zoo …	**lo zoo?** lo *dzo*·o

(At) what time does … start?	**A che ora inizia…** ah keh *o*·rah ee·*neet*·seeah
… the concert …	**il concerto?** il con·*chair*·to
… the match/game …	**l'incontro?** leen·*con*·tro
… the movie …	**il film?** il feelm
… the play …	**la commedia?** la com·*meh*·deeah
… the race …	**la corsa?** la *cor*·sah
… the show …	**lo spettacolo?** lo spet·*tah*·colo
How much is it …	**Quanto costa…** *quan*·to *cos*·tah
… for an adult?	**per un adulto?** pair oon a·*dool*·to
… for a child?	**per un bambino?** pair oon bam·*bee*·no
Two adults, please.	**Due adulti, per favore.** *doo*·eh a·*dool*·tee pair fa·*vo*·reh
Three children, please.	**Tre bambini, per favore.** treh bam·*bee*·nee pair fa·*vo*·reh
Orchestra/balcony.	**Platea/galleria.** pla·*teh*·ah/galle·*ree*·ah
Do you have …	**Avete…** a·*veh*·teh
… a guidebook?	**una guida?** *oo*·na goo·*ee*·dah
… a program?	**un programma?** oon pro·*grahm*·mah
Where is the restroom, please?	**Dov'è il bagno, per favore?** do·*veh* il *bahn*·yo pair fa·*vo*·reh
Where is the coatroom?	**Dov'è il guardaroba?** do·*veh* il guarda·*ro*·bah
I would like to take a lesson in …	**Vorrei delle lezioni…** vor·*ray* del·leh letsee·*o*·nee
… sailing.	**di vela.** dee *veh*·lah
… scuba diving.	**di nuoto sub.** dee noo·*o*·to soob

I would like to take a lesson in …	**Vorrei delle lezioni…** vor·*ray del*·leh letsee·o·nee
… skiing.	**di sci.** dee shee
… water skiing.	**di sci d'acqua.** dee shee *dah*·quah
Can I rent …	**Potrei noleggiare…** po·*tray* noled·*jah*·reh
… a boat?	**una barca?** oo·na *bar*·cah
… a fishing rod?	**una canna da pesca?** oo·na *cahn*·nah da *pes*·cah
… a lounge chair?	**una sedia a sdraio?** oo·na *seh*·deeah ah *zdrah*·yo
… some skis?	**degli sci?** *del*·yee shee
… some ski boots?	**degli scarponi da sci?** *del*·yee scar·*po*·nee da shee
… a beach umbrella?	**un ombrellone?** oon ombrel·*lo*·neh
… the necessary equipment?	**l'equipaggiamento necessario?** lequeepahdja·*men*·to neches·*sah*·reeo
How much is it …	**Quanto costa…** *quan*·to *cos*·tah
… per day/per hour?	**al giorno/all'ora?** al *jor*·no/al·*lo*·rah
Do I need a license?	**Devo avere un'autorizzazione?** *deh*·vo a·*vair*·eh oonah·ootoreetsahtsee·o·neh

Asking If Things Are Allowed

Essential Information

· The following questions can all be asked in one way in Italian: **Si può fumare qui?**

May one smoke here?
May we smoke here?
Can one smoke here?
Can we smoke here?
Is it okay to smoke here?

To save space, only the first English version ("May one …?") is given below.

What to Say

Excuse me, please.	**Mi scusi, per favore.** mee *scoo*·zee pair fa·*vo*·reh
May one …	**Si può…** see poo·*o*
… camp here?	**campeggiare qui?** camped·*jah*·reh quee
… come in?	**entrare?** en·*trah*·reh
… dance here?	**ballare qui?** bal·*lah*·reh quee
… fish here?	**pescare qui?** pes·*cah*·reh quee
… get a drink here?	**avere qualcosa da bere qui?** a·*vair*·eh qual·*co*·sah da *bair*·eh quee
… get out this way?	**uscire di qui?** oo·*shee*·reh dee quee
… get something to eat here?	**mangiare qualcosa qui?** mahn·*jah*·reh qual·*co*·sah quee
… leave one's things here?	**lasciare della roba qui?** la·*shah*·reh *del*·la *ro*·ba quee
… look around?	**guardare in giro?** guar·*dah*·reh in *jee*·ro?
… park here?	**parcheggiare qui?** parked·*jah*·reh quee
… have a picnic here?	**fare un picnic qui?** *fah*·reh oon pic·*nic* quee

May one …	**Si può…** see poo·o
… sit here?	**sedersi qui?** seh·*dair*·see quee
… smoke here?	**fumare qui?** foo·*mah*·reh quee
… swim here?	**nuotare qui?** noo·o·*tah*·reh quee
… take pictures here?	**fare una foto qui?** *fah*·reh *oo*·na *fo*·to quee
… make a telephone call here?	**telefonare qui?** telefo·*nah*·reh quee
… wait here?	**aspettare qui?** aspet·*tah*·reh quee

Likely Reactions

Yes, certainly.	**Sì, certo.** see *chair*·to
Help yourself.	**Si serva.** see *sair*·vah
I think so.	**Penso di sì.** *pen*·so dee see
Of course.	**Naturalmente.** natooral·*men*·teh
Yes, but be careful.	**Sì, ma faccia attenzione.** see mah *fah*·chah attentsee·o·neh
No, certainly not.	**Certamente no.** chairta·*men*·teh no
I don't think so.	**Credo di no.** *creh*·do dee no
Not normally.	**Normalmente no.** normal·*men*·teh no
Sorry.	**Mi dispiace.** mee deespee·*ah*·cheh

Reference

Public Notices

Signs for Drivers, Pedestrians, Shoppers, and Overnight Guests

Accendere i fari	Turn lights on
Acqua potabile	Drinking water
Affittansi	For rent
Alt	Stop
Aperto	Open
Arrivi	Arrivals
Ascensore	Elevator
Aspettare	Wait
Attenti al cane	Beware of the dog
Attenzione	Look out
Autocarri	Trucks, heavy vehicles
Auto lavaggio	Car wash
Autostrada (a pagamento)	Highway (toll)
Avanti	Go
Bagno	Bathroom
Biglietteria (a terra)	Ticket office (not on a bus)
Biglietti	Tickets
Binario	Track, platform [*railway*]
Caduta massi	Falling rocks
Caldo (C)	Hot [*water*]
Camere libere	Rooms to rent
Carabinieri	Police
Cassa	Cash register, checkout
Chiuso	Closed
Chiuso per ferie	Closed on holidays
Chiuso per turno	Closed on a rotating basis
Con pioggia/gelo/neve	Rain/ice/snow [*slippery road*]
Da affittare	For rent
Deposito bagagli	Luggage storage
Deviazione	Detour
Disporsi su una fila	Single-lane traffic
Divieto	Prohibited
Divieto di pesca	No fishing
Divieto di sosta	No parking
Divieto di transito	Road not through

Doccia	Shower
Dogana	Customs
Domani	Tomorrow
Eccetto (autobus)	Except (buses)
Entrata	Entrance
Entrata libera	Free entrance
Fermata (a richiesta)	Stop (on request)
Fine autostrada	Highway ends
Freddo (F)	Cold [*water*]
Fumatori	Smokers
Gabinetto	Restroom
Gratuito	Free
Guida	Guide(book)
Guidare lentamente	Drive slowly
Incrocio	Crossroad, intersection
Ingresso (libero)	(Free) entrance
Inizio autostrada	Highway begins
I trasgressori saranno puniti	Trespassers will be prosecuted
Lavori in corso	Construction
Libero	Free
Limite di velocità	Speed limit
Listino prezzi	Price list
Metropolitana	Subway
Moneta	Coins
Non potabile	Not for drinking
Non toccare	Do not touch
Obbligatorio l'uso delle catene	Chains mandatory [*automobile tires*]
Occupato	Busy
Offerta speciale	Special offer
Oggi	Today
Pagamento	Payment
Parcheggio	Parking
Parcheggio limitato	Restricted parking
Partenze	Departures
Passaggio a livello	Railway crossing
Pedaggio	Toll
Pedoni	Pedestrians
Pericolo	Danger
Piano (primo, secondo, terzo, terra, seminterrato)	Floor (first, second, third, ground, basement)
Polizia	Police

Portinaio	Caretaker
Precedenza	Right of way
Precedenza (alla destra)	Right of way (on the right)
Prenotazioni	Reservations
Pronto soccorso	First aid
Rallentare	Slow down
Riservato	Reserved
Sala d'attesa	Waiting room
Saldi	Sales
Scala mobile	Escalator
Scuola	School
Senso unico	One way [*street*]
Senso vietato	No entrance
Servizi	Restrooms
Signore	Ladies
Signori	Gentlemen
Silenzio	Silence
Sosta autorizzata (dalle…)	Parking permitted (at [*certain times*])
Sosta vietata	No parking
Sottopassaggio	Underpass
Spingere	Push
Strada chiusa	Road closed
Strada dissestata	Road out
Strada pericolosa	Road dangerous
Strada ristretta	Road narrows
Suonare il campanello	Ring the bell
Suonare in portineria	Ring the caretaker
Svolta	Bend [*in road*]
Tenere la destra	Keep right
Tirare	Pull
Toilette	Restroom
Ufficio informazioni	Information office
Uscita	Exit
Uscita autostrada	Highway exit
Uscita d'emergenza	Emergency exit
Vagone ristorante	Dining car
Valanghe	Avalanches
Vicolo cieco	Cul-de-sac
Vietato	Prohibited
Vietato ai cani	No dogs allowed
Vietato fumare	No smoking
Vietato il sorpasso	No passing

Vietato il transito	Road not through
Vietato il transito autocarri	Trucks prohibited
Vietato l'ingresso (veicoli)	No entrance (for vehicles)
Zona disco orario	Hourly meter parking
Zona pedonale	Pedestrian zone
Zona slavine	Avalanche area

Abbreviations

a.C.	**avanti Cristo**	before Christ (B.C.)
ACI	**Automobile Club d'Italia**	Italian Automobile Club
AGIP	**Azienda Generale Italiana Petroli**	a chain of gas stations
alb.	**albergo**	hotel
alt.	**altezza**	height
A.N.A.S.	**Azienda Nazionale Autonoma delle Strade**	State Highway Authority
avv.	**avvocato**	attorney
C.I.T.	**Compagnia Italiana Turismo**	Italian Travel Agency
c.m.	**corrente mese**	current month
C.R.I.	**Croce Rossa Italiana**	Italian Red Cross
d.C.	**dopo Cristo**	after Christ (A.D.)
dott.	**dottore**	doctor [*medical or university graduate*]
E.A.	**ente autonomo**	local board
E.I.	**Esercito Italiano**	Italian Army
E.N.I.T.	**Ente Nazionale Italiano per il Turismo**	Italian State Tourist Authority
fatt.	**fattura**	invoice
Ferr.	**ferrovia**	railway
F.S.	**Ferrovie dello Stato**	State Railways
G.d.F.	**Guardia di Finanza**	customs officer
h	**ora**	hour
ht	**ettogrammo**	100 grams
ing.	**ingegnere**	engineer
INAM	**Istituto Nazionale Assicurazione Malattie**	National Health Insurance
I.V.A.	**Imposta sul Valore Aggiunto**	VAT (value-added tax)
L.st.	**Lire sterline**	£ sterling (English pounds)
naz.	**nazionale**	national
PP.TT.	**Poste e Telecomunicazioni**	post office

P.S.	**Pubblica Sicurezza**	police
P.T.	**Posta e Telegrafi**	post office
racc.	**raccomandata**	registered letter
RAI	**Radio Audizione Italiana**	Italian Broadcasting Company
Sig.	**Signore**	Mr.
Sig.na	**Signorina**	Miss
Sig.ra	**Signora**	Mrs.
S.p.A.	**Società per Azioni**	corporation
succ.	**succursale**	branch (office)
tel	**telefono**	telephone
V.le	**viale**	Avenue
V.U.	**Vigile Urbano**	traffic police

Numbers

Cardinal Numbers

0	**zero**	*dzai*·ro
1	**uno**	*oo*·no
2	**due**	*doo*·eh
3	**tre**	treh
4	**quattro**	*quaht*·tro
5	**cinque**	*chin*·queh
6	**sei**	say
7	**sette**	*set*·teh
8	**otto**	*ot*·to
9	**nove**	*no*·veh
10	**dieci**	dee·*eh*·chee
11	**undici**	*oon*·deechee
12	**dodici**	*do*·deechee
13	**tredici**	*treh*·deechee
14	**quattordici**	quaht·*tor*·deechee
15	**quindici**	*quin*·deechee
16	**sedici**	*seh*·deechee
17	**diciassette**	deechas·*set*·teh
18	**diciotto**	dee·*chot*·to
19	**diciannove**	dee·chan·*no*·veh
20	**venti**	*ven*·tee
21	**ventuno**	ven·*too*·no
22	**ventidue**	ventee·*doo*·eh

23	**ventitré**	ventee·*treh*
24	**ventiquattro**	ventee·*quaht*·tro
25	**venticinque**	ventee·*chin*·queh
26	**ventisei**	ventee·*say*
27	**ventisette**	ventee·*set*·teh
28	**ventotto**	ven·*tot*·to
29	**ventinove**	ventee·*no*·veh
30	**trenta**	*tren*·tah

Numbers above 30 follow the pattern of **venti**: keep the final vowel except with 1 and 8.

31	**trentuno**	tren·*too*·no
35	**trentacinque**	trenta·*chin*·queh
38	**trentotto**	tren·*tot*·to
40	**quaranta**	qua·*rahn*·tah
41	**quarantuno**	quaran·*too*·no
45	**quarantacinque**	quarantah·*chin*·queh
48	**quarantotto**	quaran·*tot*·to
50	**cinquanta**	chin·*quahn*·tah
55	**cinquantacinque**	chinquantah·*chin*·queh
60	**sessanta**	ses·*sahn*·tah
65	**sessantacinque**	sessanta·*chin*·queh
70	**settanta**	set·*tahn*·tah
80	**ottanta**	ot·*tahn*·tah
90	**novanta**	no·*vahn*·tah
100	**cento**	*chen*·to
101	**centouno**	chento·*oo*·no
102	**centodue**	chento·*doo*·eh
125	**centoventicinque**	chentoventee·*chin*·queh
150	**centocinquanta**	chentochin·*quahn*·tah
175	**centosettantacinque**	chentosettantah·*chin*·queh
200	**duecento**	doo·eh·*chen*·to
300	**trecento**	treh·*chen*·to
400	**quattrocento**	quahttro·*chen*·to
500	**cinquecento**	chinqueh·*chen*·to
1,000	**mille**	*meel*·leh
1,500	**millecinquecento**	meellehchinqueh·*chen*·to
2,000	**duemila**	dooeh·*mee*·lah
5,000	**cinquemila**	chinqueh·*mee*·lah
10,000	**diecimila**	dee·ehchee·*mee*·lah
100,000	**centomila**	chento·*mee*·lah
1,000,000	**un milione**	oon meel·*yo*·neh

Ordinal Numbers

1st	**primo (1°)**	*pree*·mo
2nd	**secondo (2°)**	se·*con*·do
3rd	**terzo (3°)**	*tairt*·so
4th	**quarto (4°)**	*quar*·to
5th	**quinto (5°)**	*queen*·to
6th	**sesto (6°)**	*ses*·to
7th	**settimo (7°)**	*set*·teemo
8th	**ottavo (8°)**	ot·*tah*·vo
9th	**nono (9°)**	*no*·no
10th	**decimo (10°)**	*deh*·cheemo
11th	**undicesimo (11°)**	oondee·*cheh*·zeemo
12th	**dodicesimo (12°)**	dodee·*cheh*·zeemo

Time

What time is it?
Che ora è?
keh *o*·rah eh

It is one o'clock.
È l'una.
eh *loo*·nah

It is …
Sono…
so·no

… two o'clock …
le due
leh *doo*·eh

… three o'clock …
le tre
leh treh

… four o'clock …
le quattro
le *quaht*·tro

… in the morning.
di mattino.
dee mat·*tee*·no

… in the afternoon.
di pomeriggio.
dee pome·*reed*·jo

… in the evening.
di sera.
dee *sair*·ah

… at night.
di notte.
dee *not*·teh

It is …
È…
eh

… noon.
mezzogiorno.
medzo·*jor*·no

… midnight.
mezzanotte.
medza·*not*·teh

It is …
Sono…
so·no

… five past five.
le cinque e cinque.
leh *chin*·queh eh *chin*·queh

… ten past five.
le cinque e dieci.
leh *chin*·queh eh dee·*eh*·chee

… a quarter past five.
le cinque e un quarto.
leh *chin*·queh eh oon *quar*·to

… twenty past five.
le cinque e venti.
leh *chin*·queh eh *ven*·tee

… twenty-five past five.
le cinque e venticinque.
leh *chin*·queh eh ventee·*chin*·queh

… half past five.
le cinque e mezza.
leh *chin*·queh eh *med*·za

… twenty-five to six.
le sei meno venticinque.
leh say *meh*·no ventee·*chin*·queh

… twenty to six.
le sei meno venti.
leh say *meh*·no *ven*·tee

… a quarter to six.
le sei meno un quarto.
leh say *meh*·no oon *quar*·to

… ten to six.
le sei meno dieci.
leh say *meh*·no dee·*eh*·chee

… five to six.
le sei meno cinque.
leh say *meh*·no *chin*·queh

(At) what time (does the train leave)?
A che ora (parte il treno)?
ah keh *o*·rah (*par*·teh il *treh*·no)

At …
Alle…
al·leh

… 13:00.
tredici.
treh·deechee

… 14:05.
quattordici e cinque.
quaht·*tor*·deechee eh *chin*·queh

… 15:10.
quindici e dieci.
quin·deechee eh dee·*eh*·chee

… 16:15.
sedici e quindici.
seh·deechee eh *quin*·deechee

… 17:20.
diciassette e venti.
deechas·*set*·teh eh *ven*·tee

… 18:25.
diciotto e venticinque.
dee·*chot*·to eh ventee·*chin*·queh

… 19:30.
diciannove e trenta.
dichan·*no*·veh eh *tren*·tah

… 20:35.
venti e trenta cinque.
ven·tee eh trenta·*chin*·queh

At …	Alle…
	al·leh
… 21:40.	**ventuno e quaranta.**
	ven·*too*·no eh qua·*rahn*·tah
… 22:45.	**ventidue e quarantacinque.**
	ventee·*doo*·eh eh
	quarantah·*chin*·queh
… 23:50.	**ventitré e cinquanta.**
	ventee·*treh* eh chin·*quahn*·tah
… 0:55.	**zero e cinquantacinque.**
	dzair·o eh chinquanta·*chin*·queh
In ten minutes.	**Fra dieci minuti.**
	fra dee·*eh*·chee mee·*noo*·tee
In a quarter of an hour.	**Fra un quarto d'ora.**
	fra oon *quar*·to *do*·rah
In half an hour.	**Fra mezz'ora.**
	fra med·*zo*·rah
In three quarters of an hour.	**Fra tre quarti d'ora.**
	fra treh *quar*·tee *do*·rah

Days

Monday	**lunedì**
	looneh·*dee*
Tuesday	**martedì**
	marteh·*dee*
Wednesday	**mercoledì**
	maircoleh·*dee*
Thursday	**giovedì**
	joveh·*dee*
Friday	**venerdì**
	venair·*dee*
Saturday	**sabato**
	sah·bato
Sunday	**domenica**
	do·*mehn*·eecah
last Monday	**lunedì scorso**
	looneh·*dee* scor·so
next Tuesday	**martedì prossimo**
	marteh·*dee* pros·seemo
on Wednesday	**mercoledì**
	maircoleh·*dee*
on Thursdays	**al giovedì**
	al joveh·*dee*

until Friday	**fino a venerdì** *fee*·no ah venair·*dee*
before Saturday	**prima di sabato** *pree*·ma dee *sah*·bato
after Sunday	**dopo domenica** *do*·po do·*mehn*·eecah
the day before yesterday	**l'altro ieri** *lahl*·tro *yair*·ee
two days ago	**due giorni fa** *doo*·eh *jor*·nee fah
yesterday	**ieri** *yair*·ee
yesterday morning	**ieri mattina** *yair*·ee mat·*tee*·nah
yesterday afternoon	**ieri pomeriggio** *yair*·ee pomai·*reed*·jo
last night	**ieri sera** *yair*·ee *seh*·rah
today	**oggi** *od*·jee
this morning	**questa mattina** *ques*·tah mat·*tee*·nah
this afternoon	**questo pomeriggio** *ques*·to pomai·*reed*·jo
tonight	**questa sera** *ques*·ta *seh*·rah
tomorrow morning	**domani mattina** do·*mah*·nee mat·*tee*·nah
tomorrow afternoon	**domani pomeriggio** do·*mah*·nee pomai·*reed*·jo
tomorrow evening/night	**domani sera** do·*mah*·nee *seh*·rah
the day after tomorrow	**dopo domani** *do*·po do·*mah*·nee

Months, Dates, Seasons, and Years

January	**gennaio** jen·*nah*·yo
February	**febbraio** feb·*brah*·yo
March	**marzo** *mart*·so

April	**aprile** a·*pree*·leh
May	**maggio** *mahd*·jo
June	**giugno** *joon*·yo
July	**luglio** *lool*·yo
August	**agosto** a·*gos*·to
September	**settembre** set·*tem*·breh
October	**ottobre** ot·*to*·breh
November	**novembre** no·*vem*·breh
December	**dicembre** dee·*chem*·breh
in January	**in gennaio** in jen·*nah*·yo
until February	**fino a febbraio** *fee*·no ah feb·*brah*·yo
before March	**prima di marzo** *pree*·ma dee *mart*·so
after April	**dopo aprile** *do*·po a·*pree*·leh
during May	**durante il mese maggio / in maggio** doo·*rahn*·teh il *mai*·seh *mahd*·jo / in *mahd*·jo
not until June	**non fino a giugno** non *fee*·no ah *joon*·yo
the beginning of July	**l'inizio di luglio** li·*neet*·seeo dee *lool*·yo
the middle of August	**la metà di agosto** la meh·*tah* dee a·*gos*·to
the end of September	**la fine di settembre** la *fee*·neh dee set·*tem*·breh
last month	**il mese scorso** il *meh*·zeh *scor*·so
this month	**questo mese** *ques*·to *meh*·zeh
next month	**il mese prossimo** il *meh*·zeh *pros*·seemo

in spring	**in primavera**	
	in preema·*vair*·ah	
in summer	**in estate**	
	in es·*tah*·teh	
in autumn	**in autunno**	
	in ah·oo·*toon*·no	
in winter	**in inverno**	
	in in·*vair*·no	
this year	**quest'anno**	
	quest·*ahn*·no	
last year	**l'anno scorso**	
	lahn·no *scor*·so	
next year	**l'anno prossimo**	
	lahn·no *pros*·seemo	
in 1995	**nel mille novecento novanta cinque**	
	nel *meel*·leh noveh·*chen*·to no·*vahn*·tah *chin*·queh	
in 2000	**nel duemila**	
	nel doo·eh·*mee*·lah	
in 2005	**nel duemila cinque**	
	nel doo·eh·*mee*·lah *chin*·queh	
What is the date today?	**Qual'è la data di oggi?**	
	quah·*leh* la *dah*·tah dee *od*·jee	
It is the 6th of March.	**È il sei di marzo.**	
	eh il say dee *mart*·so	
It is the 12th of April.	**È il dodici di aprile.**	
	eh il *do*·deechee dee a·*pree*·leh	
It is the 21st of August.	**È il ventuno di agosto.**	
	eh il ven·*too*·no dee a·*gos*·to	

Public Holidays

Banks, post offices, public offices, retail stores, and schools are closed on the following holidays.

1 January	**Primo dell'anno / Capodanno**	New Year's Day
6 January	**Epifania**	Feast of the Epiphany
[*varies*]	**Lunedì dell'Angelo**	Easter Monday
25 April	**Festa della Liberazione**	Liberation Day
1 May	**Festa del Lavoro**	Labor Day
15 August	**Assunzione**	Assumption Day
1 November	**Tutti i Santi**	All Saints Day

2 November	**Tutti i Morti**	All Souls Day [*in some parts of Italy*]
8 December	**Immacolata Concezione**	Immaculate Conception
25 December	**Natale**	Christmas
26 December	**Santo Stefano**	Feast of St. Stephen

Countries and Nationalities

Countries

Australia
(l')Australia
(l)ah·oo·*strahl*·yah

Austria
(l')Austria
(l)ah·*oos*·treeah

Belgium
(il) Belgio
(il) *bel*·jo

Britain
(la) Gran Bretagna
(la) grahn breh·*tahn*·yah

Canada
(il) Canada
(il) *cah*·nadah

East Africa
(l')Africa Est
(l)ah·fricah est

Eire
(l')Eire
(l)eh·ee·reh

England
(l')Inghilterra
(l) ingheel·*tair*·ah

France
(la) Francia
(la) *frahn*·chah

Germany
(la) Germania
(la) jair·*mahn*·yah

Greece
(la) Grecia
(la) *grai*·chah

India
(l')India
(l)*een*·deeah

Italy
(l')Italia
(l)i·*tahl*·yah

Luxembourg
(il) Lussemburgo
(il) loossem·*boor*·go

Netherlands
(i) Paesi Bassi
(ee) pah·*eh*·zee *bahs*·see

New Zealand
(la) Nuova Zelanda
(la) noo·*o*·vah zai·*lahn*·dah

Northern Ireland
(l')Irlanda del Nord
(l)eer·*lahn*·dah del nord

Pakistan	**(il) Pakistan**
	(il) pakis·*tahn*
Portugal	**(il) Portogallo**
	(il) porto·*gal*·lo
Scotland	**(la) Scozia**
	(la) *scot*·seeah
South Africa	**(il) Sudafrica**
	(il) soo·*dah*·fricah
Spain	**(la) Spagna**
	(la) *spahn*·ya
Switzerland	**(la) Svizzera**
	(la) *zveet*·serah
United States	**(gli) Stati Uniti**
	(l·yee) *stah*·tee oo·*nee*·tee
Wales	**(il) Galles**
	(il) *gahl*·les
West Indies	**(le) Indie Occidentali**
	(leh) een·dee·eh ochiden·*tah*·lee

Nationalities

Where two alternatives are given, the first is used for males, the second for females.

American	**americano/americana**
	ameri·*cah*·no/ameri·*cah*·nah
Australian	**australiano/australiana**
	ah·oostrahl·*yah*·no/
	ah·oostrahl·*yah*·nah
Canadian	**canadese**
	cana·*dai*·zeh
East African	**est africano/est africana**
	est afri·*cah*·no/est afri·*cah*·nah
English/British	**inglese**
	in·*glai*·zeh
French	**francese**
	fran·*cheh*·zeh
German	**tedesco/tedesca**
	te·*des*·co/te·*des*·cah
Indian	**indiano/indiana**
	in·dee·*ah*·no/in·dee·*ah*·nah
Irish	**irlandese**
	eerlan·*dai*·zeh
New Zealander	**neozelandese**
	nai·odzelan·*dai*·zeh

Pakistani	**pachistano/pachistana** pakis·*tah*·no/pakis·*tah*·nah
Scots	**scozzese** scot·*sai*·zeh
South African	**sudafricano/sudafricana** soodafri·*cah*·no/soodafri·*cah*·nah
Welsh	**gallese** gal·*lai*·zeh
West Indian	**indiano occidentale/** **indiana occidentale** in·dee·*ah*·no ochiden·*tah*·leh/ in·dee·*ah*·nah ochiden·*tah*·leh

Department Store Guide

Abbigliamento e accessori **neonato-bambini**	Infants/children's department
Abbigliamento e attrezzi **sportive**	Sports clothing and equipment
Abbigliamento donna	Ladies' fashions
Abbigliamento uomo	Men's fashions
Accessori auto	Automobile accessories
Accessori bagno	Bathroom accessories
Alimentari	Food
Arredamento (cucine)	Furnishings (kitchen)
Articoli da campeggio	Camping equipment
Articoli casalinghi	Household articles
Articoli fotografici	Photography supplies
Articoli da fumo	Smoking supplies
Articoli da pesca	Fishing equipment
Articoli da pulizia	Cleaning materials
Articoli da regalo	Gifts
Articoli per ufficio	Office equipment
Articoli da viaggio	Travel items
Biancheria	Linens
Borse/borsette	Purses, handbags
Bricolage	Do-it-yourself
Calzature	Shoes
Calze	Stockings, socks
Camicette	Blouses
Camicie	Shirts
Cartoleria	Stationery
CDs	Compact discs

Cinture	Belts
Coperte	Blankets
Corsetteria	Underwear
Cosmetici	Cosmetics
Cotoni	Cottons
Cravatte	Ties
Cristalleria	Crystal ware
Dischi	Phonograph records
Elettrodomestici	Electrical appliances
Ferramenta	Hardware
Fotocopie	Photocopies
Foulards	Scarves
Giocattoli	Toys
Gioielli	Jewelry
Gonne	Skirts
Guanti	Gloves
Impermeabili	Raincoats
Lana	Wool [*knitting yarn*]
Libri	Books
Maglieria	Knitwear
Mare	Beachwear
Maternità	Maternity
Mercerie	Notions
Mobili	Furniture
Moda giovane	Youth fashions
Modisteria	Millinery, hats
Ombrelli	Umbrellas
Orologi	Watches
Pantaloni	Trousers
Pellicceria	Furs
Piano	Floor
Porcellane	Porcelain
Portafogli	Wallets
Primo piano	First floor
Profumeria	Perfumes
Quarto piano	Fourth floor
Radio-televisori	Radio/television
Ristorante	Restaurant
Sciarpe	Scarves
Secondo piano	Second floor
Seminterrato	Basement
Tacchi espresso–chiavi	Shoe heel repair/key duplication

Taglie forti	Plus sizes
Tappeti	Carpet, rugs
Tende	Curtains
Terzo piano	Third floor
Tessuti	Fabrics
Ufficio informazioni	Information desk
Ufficio vendite a credito	Credit sales department
Ufficio viaggi	Travel agency
Vetro-ceramica	Glassware, china

Conversion Tables

Metric/U.S. systems

To convert from the metric to the U.S. system, read from the single digit in the center column to the number on the left; for example, 5 liters = 10.55 pints. To convert from the U.S. system to the metric, read from the single digit in the center column to the number on the right; for example, 5 pints = 2.35 liters.

PINTS		LITERS	GALLONS		LITERS
2.11	1	0.47	0.26	1	3.79
4.23	2	0.95	0.53	2	7.57
6.34	3	1.42	0.79	3	11.36
8.45	4	1.89	1.06	4	15.14
10.57	5	2.37	1.32	5	18.93
12.68	6	2.84	1.59	6	22.71
14.79	7	3.31	1.85	7	26.50
16.91	8	3.79	2.11	8	30.28
19.02	9	4.26	2.38	9	34.07

OUNCES		GRAMS	POUNDS		KILOS
0.04	1	28.35	2.20	1	0.45
0.07	2	56.70	4.41	2	0.91
0.11	3	85.05	6.61	3	1.36
0.14	4	113.40	8.82	4	1.81
0.18	5	141.75	11.02	5	2.27
0.21	6	170.10	13.23	6	2.72
0.25	7	198.45	15.43	7	3.18
0.28	8	226.80	17.64	8	3.63
0.32	9	255.15	19.84	9	4.08

INCHES		CENTIMETERS	YARDS		METERS
0.39	1	2.54	1.09	1	0.91
0.79	2	5.08	2.19	2	1.83
1.18	3	7.62	3.28	3	2.74
1.58	4	10.16	4.37	4	3.66
1.97	5	12.70	5.47	5	4.57
2.36	6	15.24	6.56	6	5.49
2.76	7	17.78	7.66	7	6.40
3.15	8	20.32	8.75	8	7.32
3.54	9	22.86	9.84	9	8.23

MILES		KILOMETERS
0.62	1	1.61
1.24	2	3.22
1.86	3	4.83
2.49	4	6.44
3.11	5	8.05
3.73	6	9.66
4.35	7	11.27
4.97	8	12.88
5.59	9	14.48

To quickly convert kilometers to miles, divide by 8 and multiply by 5.
To quickly convert miles to kilometers, divide by 5 and multiply by 8.

Temperature

FAHRENHEIT ($°F$)	CELSIUS ($°C$)	
212°	100°	boiling point of water
100°	38°	
98.6°	37°	body temperature
86°	30°	
77°	25°	
68°	20°	
59°	15°	
50°	10°	
41°	5°	
32°	0°	freezing point of water
14°	−10°	
−4°	−20°	

To convert degrees Celsius to degrees Fahrenheit, divide by 5, multiply by 9, and add 32. To convert degrees Fahrenheit to degrees Celsius: subtract 32, divide by 9, and multiply by 5.

Tire Pressure

POUNDS PER SQUARE INCH	KILOGRAMS PER SQUARE CENTIMETER
18	1.3
20	1.4
22	1.5
25	1.8
29	2.0
32	2.2
35	2.5
36	2.5
39	2.7
40	2.8
43	3.0
45	3.2
46	3.2
50	3.5
60	4.2

Clothing Sizes

Always try clothes on before buying. Clothing sizes in conversion tables are often unreliable.

Women's Dresses and Suits

Continental Europe	38	40	42	44	46	48
U.K.	32	34	36	38	40	42
U.S.	10	12	14	16	18	20

Men's Suits, Coats, and Jackets

Continental Europe	46	48	50	52	54	56
U.K./U.S.	36	38	40	42	44	46

Men's Shirts

Continental Europe	36	37	38	39	41	42	43
U.K./U.S.	14	14½	15	15½	16	16½	17

Socks

Continental Europe	38–39	39–40	40–41	41–42	42–43
U.K./U.S.	9½	10	10½	11	11½

Shoes

Continental Europe	34	35½	36½	38	39
U.K.	2	3	4	5	6
U.S.	3½	4½	5½	6½	7½

Continental Europe	41	42	43	44	45
U.K.	7	8	9	10	11
U.S.	8½	9½	10½	11½	12½

Do It Yourself: Some Notes on the Italian Language

This section does not deal with "grammar" as such. The purpose here is to explain some of the most obvious and elementary nuts and bolts of the language, based on the principal phrases included in the book. This information should enable you to produce numerous sentences of your own making.

There is no pronunciation guide in most of this section, partly because it would get in the way of the explanations and partly because you have to do it yourself at this stage if you are serious. You can use the earlier examples in this book to figure out the pronunciation of the Italian words in this section.

"The"

All nouns in Italian belong to one of two genders—masculine or feminine—regardless of whether they refer to living beings or inanimate objects.

"the" (SINGULAR)	MASCULINE	FEMININE
the address	l'indirizzo	
the apple		la mela
the bill	il conto	
the cup of tea		la tazza di tè
the glass of wine	il bicchiere di vino	
the key		la chiave
the menu	il menù	
the newspaper	il giornale	
the receipt		la ricevuta
the sandwich	il panino	
the suitcase		la valigia
the telephone directory		la guida telefonica
the timetable	l'orario	
the travel agency		l'agenzia di viaggi
the zoo	lo zoo	

- "The" is **il** before most masculine nouns and **la** before most feminine nouns.

- "The" is **lo** before certain masculine nouns because of the way the nouns are spelled, especially those that begin with *z*, for example, **lo zoo**.

- "The" is **l'** before masculine and feminine nouns that begin with a vowel, for example, **l'indirizzo** (masculine) and **l'agenzia** (feminine).

- You can often predict if a singular noun is masculine or feminine by its ending. Masculine nouns usually end in *o*, and feminine nouns in *a*. But there are many exceptions, notably an entire group of nouns that end in *e*, for example, **il giornale**, so you should learn the gender of nouns as you learn the nouns themselves. If you read a word with **il**, **lo**, or **la** in front of it, you can detect its gender immediately: **il menu** and **lo zoo** are masculine (*m.* or *masc.* in dictionaries), and **la valigia** is feminine (*f.* or *fem.* in dictionaries).

- Does it matter? Not unless you want to make a serious attempt to speak correctly and scratch beneath the surface of the language. You would be understood if you said **la menù** or even **il agenzia**, provided your pronunciation was good.

"the" (PLURAL)	MASCULINE	FEMININE
the addresses	**gli indirizzi**	
the apples		**le mele**
the bills	**i conti**	
the cups of tea		**le tazze di tè**
the glasses of wine	**i bicchieri di vino**	
the keys		**le chiavi**
the luggage	**i bagagli**	
the menus	**i menù**	
the newspapers	**i giornali**	
the receipts		**le ricevute**
the sandwiches	**i panini**	
the suitcases		**le valigie**
the telephone directories		**le guide telefoniche**
the timetables	**gli orari**	
the travel agencies		**le agenzie di viaggi**
the zoos	**gli zoo**	

- Most masculine plural nouns end in *i,* and most feminine plural nouns end in *e.*

- "The" is **i** before most masculine nouns in the plural. Masculine nouns whose singular forms use **l'** or **lo** for "the," use **gli** in the plural.

- "The" is **le** before all feminine nouns in the plural.

- In Italian, "luggage" is always regarded as plural. It is never used to mean an individual piece of luggage.

Practice saying and writing the following sentences in Italian. Note that there are two ways of saying "do you have" politely in Italian: **ha** (when speaking to one person) and **avete** (when speaking to more than one person or in formal settings, such as in a hotel, store, or tourist information office).

Do you have the keys?	**Avete le chiavi?**
Do you have the luggage?	**Avete...?**
Do you have the telephone directory?	**Ha...?**
Do you have the menu?	
I would like the key.	**Vorrei la chiave.**
I would like the receipt.	**Vorrei....**
I would like the bill.	
I would like the keys.	
Where is the key?	**Dov'è la chiave?**
Where is the timetable?	**Dov'è...?**
Where is the address?	
Where is the zoo?	
Where is the suitcase?	
Where is the travel agency?	
Where are the keys?	**Dove sono le chiavi?**
Where are the sandwiches?	**Dove sono...?**
Where are the apples?	
Where are the suitcases?	
Where is the luggage?	**Dove sono ...?**
Where can I get the key?	**Dove posso trovare la chiave?**
Where can I get the address?	**Dove posso trovare...?**
Where can I get the timetables?	

Now try to make up more sentences along the same lines. Try adding "please" (**per favore**) at the end.

"A"/"An" and "Some"/"Any"

"a"/"an" (SINGULAR)	MASCULINE	FEMININE
an address	un indirizzo	
an apple		una mela
a bill	un conto	
a cup of tea		una tazza di tè
a glass of wine	un bicchiere di vino	
a key		una chiave
a menu	un menù	
a newspaper	un giornale	
a receipt		una ricevuta
a sandwich	un sandwich	
a suitcase		una valigia
a telephone directory		una guida telefonica
a timetable	un orario	
a travel agency		un'agenzia di viaggi
a zoo	uno zoo	

"some"/"any" (PLURAL)	MASCULINE	FEMININE
addresses	degli indirizzi	
apples		delle mele
bills	dei conti	
cups of tea		delle tazze di tè
glasses of wine	dei bicchieri di vino	
keys		delle chiavi
luggage	dei bagagli	
menus	dei menù	
newspapers	dei giornali	
receipts		delle ricevute
sandwiches	dei panini	
suitcases		delle valigie
telephone directories		delle guide telefoniche
timetables	degli orari	
travel agencies		delle agenzie di viaggi
zoos	degli zoo	

- "A" or "an" is **un** before most masculine nouns and **una** before most feminine nouns.

- Before the group of masculine nouns that start with *z*, "a" or "an" is **uno**.

- Before feminine nouns that begin with a vowel, "a" or "an" is **un'**.

- "Some" or "any" is **dei** before most masculine plural nouns and **delle** before all feminine plural nouns.

- Before masculine plural nouns that begin with a vowel or that belong to the **z** group, "some" or "any" is **degli**.

- In certain Italian expressions, **dei**, **delle**, and **degli** are omitted, for example, after the preposition **di**. Examples of this are marked by an asterisk (*) before some of the sentences below.

Practice saying and writing the following sentences in Italian.

Do you have a receipt?	**Ha una ricevuta?**
Do you have a menu?	**Ha...?**
I would like a telephone directory.	**Vorrei....**
I would like some sandwiches.	
Where can I get some newspapers?	**Dove posso trovare...?**
Where can I get a cup of tea?	
Is there a key?	**C'è una chiave?**
Is there a telephone directory?	**C'è...?**
Is there a timetable?	
Is there a menu?	
Is there a zoo?	
Is there a travel agency?	
Are there any keys?	**Ci sono delle chiavi?**
Are there any newspapers?	**Ci sono dei...?**
Are there any sandwiches?	

Now make up your own sentences along the same lines.

Try the following new phrases.

I'll have ...	**Io prendo...**
I need ...	**Avrei bisogno di...**
I'll have a glass of wine.	**Io prendo un bicchiere di vino.**
I'll have a cup of tea.	**Io prendo....**
I'll have some sandwiches.	
I'll have some apples.	
I need a cup of tea.	**Avrei bisogno di una tazza di tè.**
I need a key.	**Avrei bisogno di....**
*I need some newspapers.	**Avrei bisogno di giornali.**
*I need some keys.	**Avrei bisogno di...**
*I need some addresses.	
*I need some sandwiches.	
*I need some suitcases.	

In cases where "some" or "any" refers to more than one thing, such as *some/any ice creams, some/any sunglasses,* and *some/any bananas,* **dei**, **degli**, and **delle** are used as explained above.

some/any ice cream	**dei gelati**
some/any sunglasses	**degli occhiali da sole**
some/any bananas	**delle banane**

As a guide, you can usually *count* the number of containers or whole items.

In cases where "some" refers to part of a whole thing or an indefinite quantity, the words **dei**, **degli**, and **delle** are not used.

the bread	**il pane**	some bread	**del pane**
the flour	**la farina**	some flour	**della farina**
the oil	**l'olio** (*masc.*)	some oil	**dell'olio**
the sugar	**lo zucchero**	some sugar	**dello zucchero**
the water	**l'acqua** (*fem.*)	some water	**dell'acqua**
the wine	**il vino**	some wine	**del vino**

- The noun in these cases is always singular.
- **Del** is generally used before masculine nouns, and **della** is generally used before feminine nouns.
- **Dell'** is used before both masculine and feminine nouns that begin with a vowel.
- **Dello** is used before masculine nouns that begin with **z**.

Can you complete the list below?

the aspirin	**l'aspirina**	some aspirin	_____
the beer	**la birra**	some beer	_____
the cheese	**il formaggio**	some cheese	_____
the coffee	**il caffè**	some coffee	_____
the lemonade	**la limonata**	some lemonade	_____
the tea	**il tè**	some tea	_____

Practice saying and writing the following sentences in Italian.

Do you have some coffee?	**Avete del caffè?**
Do you have some flour?	
Do you have some sugar?	
I would like some aspirin.	**Vorrei dell'aspirina.**
I would like some oil.	
I would like some bread.	

Is there any lemonade?	**C'è della limonata?**
Is there any water?	
Is there any wine?	
Where can I get some cheese?	**Dove posso trovare del formaggio?**
Where can I get some flour?	
I'll have some beer.	**Io prendo della birra.**
I'll have some tea.	
I'll have some coffee.	

"This" and "That"

Italian uses **questo** for "this" and **quello** for "that." If you do not know the Italian word for something, just point to the object and say the following.

I would like that.	**Vorrei quello.**
I'll have that.	**Prendo quello.**
I need this.	**Avrei bisogno di questo.**

Helping Others

You can help yourself by using sentences such as the following.

I would like a sandwich.	**Vorrei un panino.**
Where can I get a cup of tea?	**Dove posso trovare una tazza di tè?**
I'll have a glass of wine.	**Io prendo un bicchiere di vino.**
I need a receipt.	**Avrei bisogno di una ricevuta.**

If you encounter a speaker of English who is having trouble making himself or herself understood, you should be able to speak Italian on the person's behalf.

It is not necessary to say the words for "he" (**lui**), "she" (**lei**), and "I" (**io**) in Italian unless you want to emphasize them (as in "*He'll* have a beer, and *I'll* have a glass of wine"). The verb ending changes for "he" and "she."

He would like ….	**(Lui) vorrebbe un panino.**
	(*loo*·ee) vor·*reb*·beh oon pah·*nee*·no
She would like ….	**(Lei) vorrebbe un panino.**
	(lay) vor·*reb*·beh oon pah·*nee*·no

Where can he get …?	**Dove può trovare (lui) una tazza di tè?**
	do·veh poo·*o* tro·*vah*·reh (*loo*·ee) *oo*·na *taht*·sah dee teh
Where can she get …?	**Dove può trovare (lei) una tazza di tè?**
	do·veh poo·*o* tro·*vah*·reh (lay) *oo*·na *taht*·sah dee teh
He'll have ….	**(Lui) prende un bicchiere di vino.**
	(*loo*·ee) *pren*·deh oon beekee·*air*·eh dee *vee*·no
She'll have ….	**(Lei) prende un bicchiere di vino.**
	(lay) *pren*·deh oon beekee·*air*·eh dee *vee*·no
He needs ….	**(Lui) avrebbe bisogno di una ricevuta.**
	(*loo*·ee) av·*reb*·beh bee·*zon*·yo dee *oo*·na richeh·*voo*·tah
She needs ….	**(Lei) avrebbe bisogno di una ricevuta.**
	(lay) av·*reb*·beh bee·*zon*·yo dee *oo*·na richeh·*voo*·tah

You can also help two or more people who are having difficulties. The Italian word for "they" is **loro**, but it is usually omitted. Instead, the verb ending changes for "they."

They would like ….	**(Loro) vorrebbero del formaggio.**
	(*lo*·ro) vor·*reb*·bero del for·*mahd*·jo
Where can they get …?	**Dove possono trovare dell'aspirina?**
	do·veh *pos*·sono tro·*vah*·reh dellaspi·*ree*·nah
They'll have ….	**Prendono del vino.**
	pren·dono del *vee*·no
They need ….	**Avrebbero bisogno di acqua.**
	av·*reb*·bero bee·*zon*·yo dee *ah*·quah

What about the two of you? No problem. The word for "we" is **noi** (noy), but it is usually omitted. Instead, the verb ending changes for "we."

We would like ….	**Vorremmo del vino.**
	vor·*rem*·mo del *vee*·no
Where can we get …?	**Dove possiamo trovare dell'acqua?**
	do·veh possee·*ah*·mo tro·*vah*·reh del·*lah*·quah

We'll have ….	**Prendiamo della birra.**
	prendee·*ah*·mo *del*·la *beer*·rah
We need ….	**Avremmo bisogno di aspirina.**
	av·*rem*·mo bee·*zon*·yo dee
	aspi·*ree*·nah

Try writing out your own checklist for these four useful sentence-starters, like the following.

Vorrei….	**Vorremmo….**
Vorrebbe (lui)….	**Vorrebbero….**
Vorrebbe (lei)….	

Dove posso trovare…?	**Dove… trovare…? (noi)**
Dove può trovare (lui)…?	**Dove… trovare…? (loro)**
Dove può trovare (lei)…?	

More Practice

Here are some more Italian names of things. Using the information given above, see how many different sentences you can make up.

	SINGULAR	PLURAL
ashtray	**portacenere** (*masc.*)	**portaceneri**
car	**macchina** (*fem.*)	**macchine**
cigarette	**sigaretta** (*fem.*)	**sigarette**
corkscrew	**cavatappi** (*masc.*)	**cavatappi**
garage (repairs)	**autoriparazione** (*fem.*)	**autoriparazioni**
grapes	**uva** (*fem.*)	(*no plural*)
ice cream	**gelato** (*masc.*)	**gelati**
lounge chair	**sedia a sdraio** (*fem.*)	**sedie a sdraio**
melon	**melone** (*masc.*)	**meloni**
passport	**passaporto** (*masc.*)	**passaporti**
purse	**borsa** (*fem.*)	**borse**
rag (dishcloth)	**(lo/uno) straccio** (*masc.*)	**stracci**
salad (lettuce)	**insalata** (*fem.*)	**insalate**
shoe	**scarpa** (*fem.*)	**scarpe**
stamp	**francobollo** (*masc.*)	**francobolli**
station	**stazione** (*fem.*)	**stazioni**
sunglasses	(*no singular*)	**occhiali da sole** (*masc.*)
telephone	**telefono** (*masc.*)	**telefoni**
telephone card	**scheda telefonica** (*fem.*)	**schede telefoniche**
ticket	**biglietto** (*masc.*)	**biglietti**

Index